TURN-TO-LEARN

Word Family Wheels

32 Easy-to-Make Manipulative Wheels that Help Kids Master Key Phonograms & Become Successful Readers

Written by Liza Charlesworth • Illustrated by Rusty Fletcher

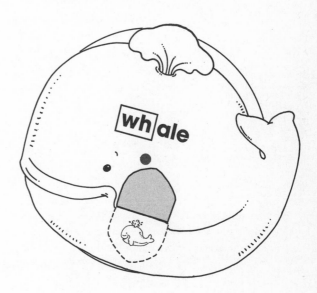

SCHOLASTIC
PROFESSIONAL BOOKS

New York • Toronto • London • Auckland • Sydney
Mexico City • New Delhi • Hong Kong

Interior design by Grafica, Inc.
Cover design by Pamela Simmons
Illustrations by Rusty Fletcher

ISBN: 0-590-64376-2

Contents

W O R D   W H E E L S

Introduction

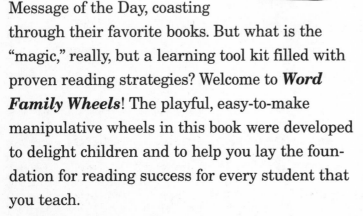

For some students, reading happens so naturally that the process seems almost magical. In no time, these children are decoding street signs, sounding out the Message of the Day, coasting through their favorite books. But what is the "magic," really, but a learning tool kit filled with proven reading strategies? Welcome to **Word Family Wheels**! The playful, easy-to-make manipulative wheels in this book were developed to delight children and to help you lay the foundation for reading success for every student that you teach.

Research shows that a knowledge of rhyming word families is an essential part of a balanced reading program. When children have repeated encounters with rhyming word families—also known as *phonograms*—they come to recognize spelling patterns, gaining the ability to decode "member" words by analogy. The ability to decode by analogy is an empowering tool because it enables students to read hundreds and hundreds of words with greater confidence and fluency.

A few minutes a day or week is all it takes to integrate word-family instruction into your school day. (In fact, some children require as little as four or five encounters with new words before they can recognize them by sight.) But which word families should you emphasize and make a

10 Reasons to Make Rhyming Word Wheels a Part of Your Reading Program

1. Rhyming word wheels will empower children to read hundreds of new words.

2. Rhyming word wheels will help children master letter sounds and blends.

3. Rhyming word wheels are easy to make and even easier to use.

4. Rhyming word wheels can be used a lot or a little—it's up to you!

5. Rhyming word wheels are self-correcting so kids can learn independently.

6. Rhyming word wheels are a natural way to reach kinesthetic learners.

7. Rhyming word wheels provide a powerful leg up for struggling readers.

8. Rhyming word wheels are great "to go," enabling children to reinforce reading skills at home with parents.

9. Rhyming word wheels show kids that literacy extends beyond books.

10. Rhyming word wheels make learning to read fun!

point of teaching? Although all phonograms are important, educators Wylie and Durrell identified 37 that are found in more than 500 primary-grade words (see sidebar). That means that exposing children to this relatively small set of word families allows them to add a huge number of words to their reading repertoire. And here's more good news: Of the 37 recommended phonograms, 32 are included here in the form of reproducible word wheels. (For the remaining five, you'll find word lists on page 10 and easy activities for teaching them on pages 8–10.)

The rhyming word wheels in this book are quick to make—just color, cut, and add a brass fastener. And they're so flexible to use: Create class sets, tuck them in backpacks to build at-home literacy, or place them in learning centers for children to explore independently. However you choose to incorporate them into your classroom routine, we have a hunch your students will enjoy—and greatly benefit from—this playful spin on reading instruction!

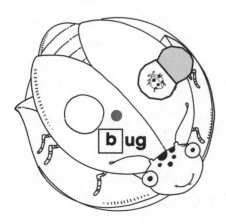

37 Key Phonograms

The phonograms not included in word wheel form are marked with an asterisk. You'll find word lists for those phonograms on page 10 and activity ideas on pages 8–10.

-ack	-ide
-ail	-ight
-ain	-ill
-ake	-in
-ale	-ine
-ame*	-ing
-an	-ink
-ank	-ip
-ap	-it*
-ash	-ock
-at	-oke*
-ate	-op
-aw	-ore*
-ay	-ot
-eat*	-uck
-ell	-ug
-est	-ump
-ice	-unk
-ick	

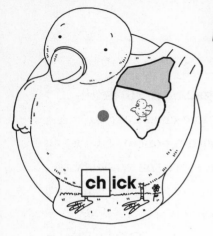

Making Rhyming Word Wheels

Materials

- paper
- scissors
- brass fasteners
- crayons or markers
- oaktag/contact paper/
  lamination machine (optional)

How-to's

Each rhyming word wheel is created from two pages: one shape wheel and one word/picture wheel. The wheels can be constructed by you, parent volunteers, or your students. Here are the easy directions:

1. Photocopy both parts of the wheel.

2. Color or invite children to color the shape wheel and the pictures on the word/picture wheel. (If you like, paste the pages to oaktag and/or laminate them for added durability.)

3. Cut out the shape and picture/word wheels. Cut out the window and door along the dashed lines.

4. Place the shape wheel on top of the word/picture wheel. Align the crosses in the center as shown.

5. Push a brass fastener through the crosses and open to secure. Now you're ready to turn to learn!

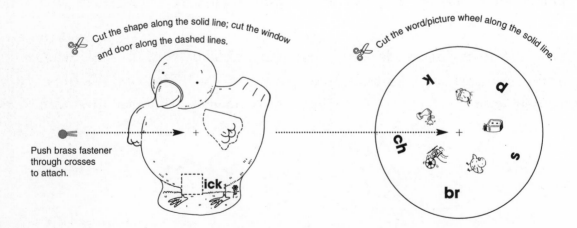

Cut the shape along the solid line; cut the window and door along the dashed lines.

Cut the word/picture wheel along the solid line.

Push brass fastener through crosses to attach.

Using Rhyming Word Wheels

There are many ways to make rhyming word wheels an engaging part of children's reading routine, both formally and informally. For whole-class instruction, provide each student with his or her own set of wheels, assigning one or two a week. (Once children have mastered a phonogram, they can store the wheel with others in a pocket folder or take each home to share with parents.) To encourage independent learning, laminate a class set. Then nest the wheels in a basket, cubby, or labeled accordion file and place it in your learning center. (**TIP:** To keep your wheels neat and tidy, try clipping them to a clothesline.)

Here are six easy steps to set the stage for learning with rhyming word wheels:

1. Demonstrate how to line up the onset (*b*) and rime (*-ack*) in the wheel's window to create a word such as *back*.

2. Invite children to sound out the word aloud and then open the flap to see if they are right by checking the picture cue.

3. Show children how to turn the wheel to create a new word (*sack*) with the old rime (*-ack*).

4. Have children spin the wheel and sound out each word as many times as you—and they—choose.

5. Extend learning by sharing additional words in the rhyming word family and doing a quick-and-easy activity from pages 8–10.

6. Keep track of each student's exposure to and mastery of the recommended 37 phonograms with the easy assessment grid on page 11.

TIP: Provide struggling readers with extra time to "play" with the word wheels. Or, send the wheels home for added practice. Parents will likely enjoy and be comfortable with this easy and fun method of developing reading skills.

Quick Activities to Extend Learning

Super Silly Sentences

Choose a phonogram such as *-at*. With students, brainstorm a long list of rhyming words (*flat, mat, that, sat, rat, cat, hat, fat*). Write them on the blackboard or on cards that can be reordered on the chalk tray. Next, challenge children to work together to make up a sentence that includes as many of the words as possible; for example: *The fat cat that sat on the mat wanted to wear the rat's flat hat.* Don't be afraid to get super silly! For added fun, ask volunteers to illustrate one or more of the sentences.

Beanbag Rhyme Toss

Support kinesthetic learners with this engaging rhyming game! Invite students to stand in a circle and toss a beanbag around. Start them off with a phonogram that is easy to rhyme, such as *bug*. Invite the child holding the beanbag to name a rhyming word (for example, *hug*) and then toss it to the student to his or her right to do the same. If a child cannot name a new rhyming word, he or she says "pass" and hands—not tosses—the beanbag to the next child. When three kids in a row say "pass," it's time to start a new game with a fresh phonogram.

Collaborative Word-Family Dictionaries

Enrich learning by publishing a class set of word-family dictionaries. Divide the class into cooperative groups, and assign each a different phonogram (*-ack, -ill, -ink, -unk,* and so on). Challenge each group of book-makers to work together to write a new rhyming word on every page (*back, sack, tack, black, shack, track*) and to illustrate them with simple pictures and then label the cover (for example, "Our -ACK Words"). When the books are complete, place them in an accessible spot for kids to turn to for friendly reading, writing, and spelling support.

Rhyme-Time Concentration

Using two or more phonogram lists for reference, jot rhyming words on index cards—one word to each card. (**TIP:** Make sure you include an even number of rhyming words in each family.) Shuffle the cards, then place them facedown in rows. Invite students to take turns turning over the cards to make matches. If two words rhyme (such as *ban* and *van*), the student gets to keep the cards and try again. Play continues until all cards have been picked up; the child with the most wins.

Go Fish-Dish-Wish!

Make a class set of about 36 playing cards, using several different rhyming word pairs. (**TIP:** You can purchase blank playing cards at many teacher stores.) Tell children that they will be using the cards to play "Go Fish-Dish-Wish." The rules of the game are the same as classic "Go Fish," except children will be looking for sets of rhyming words instead of numbers/face cards. The child with the most matches wins.

Clap and Stamp Poetry

Read aloud lots and lots of poems! Some great sources include *Poem a Day*; *Poems, Songs, and Fingerplays*; and the *Month-by-Month Classroom Poetry* series (all from Scholastic Professional Books). As you read a poem, invite children to clap and stamp each time they hear a rhyming word. (**TIP:** For more advanced students, assign a different action for each new phonogram.) This activity is a great—and meaningful—way to "shake out the sillies" during circle time.

"I Spy" Rhymes

Play a rhyming word version of "I Spy," using items in your classroom. For example, "I spy with my little eye, something that rhymes with look." (*book*) Or "I spy with my little eye, something that rhymes with moo." (*shoe*) Once children have mastered the concept, invite them to generate their own riddles to share with classmates.

Rhyming Relay Race

Divide the class into three or four teams, and have each line up. On the board, write a different word for each team—for example, *cake*, *mice*, and *duck*. (**TIP:** Make sure you select phonograms with lots of rhyming possibilities.) Next, challenge each child, in turn, to come up to the board and add a rhyming word to his or her team's list. Team members can help each other out. The team to generate the longest list is the winner!

Word Lists for Key Phonograms (Not Included as Word Wheels)

-ame	-eat	-it	-oke	-ore
came	beat	bit	coke	bore
dame	feat	fit	joke	core
fame	heat	hit	poke	lore
game	meat	kit	woke	more
lame	neat	lit	yoke	pore
name	peat	pit	broke	sore
tame	seat	quit	choke	wore
blame		sit	smoke	chore
flame		wit	stoke	shore
frame		flit	stroke	snore
shame		grit		store
		skit		
		slit		
		spit		
		split		

Easy Phonogram Assessment Grid

Student's Name _____

Phonogram	Word Wheel Play			Other Activities	Has Mastered	Needs More Practice
	1	**2**	**3**			
-ack						
-ail						
-ain						
-ake						
-ale						
-ame*						
-an						
-ank						
-ap						
-ash						
-at						
-ate						
-aw						
-ay						
-eat*						
-ell						
-est						
-ice						
-ick						
-ide						
-ight						
-ill						
-in						
-ine						
-ing						
-ink						
-ip						
-ir*						
-ock						
-oke*						
-op						
-ore*						
-ot						
-uck						
-ug						
-ump						
-unk						

Phonogram: -ack

ack

+

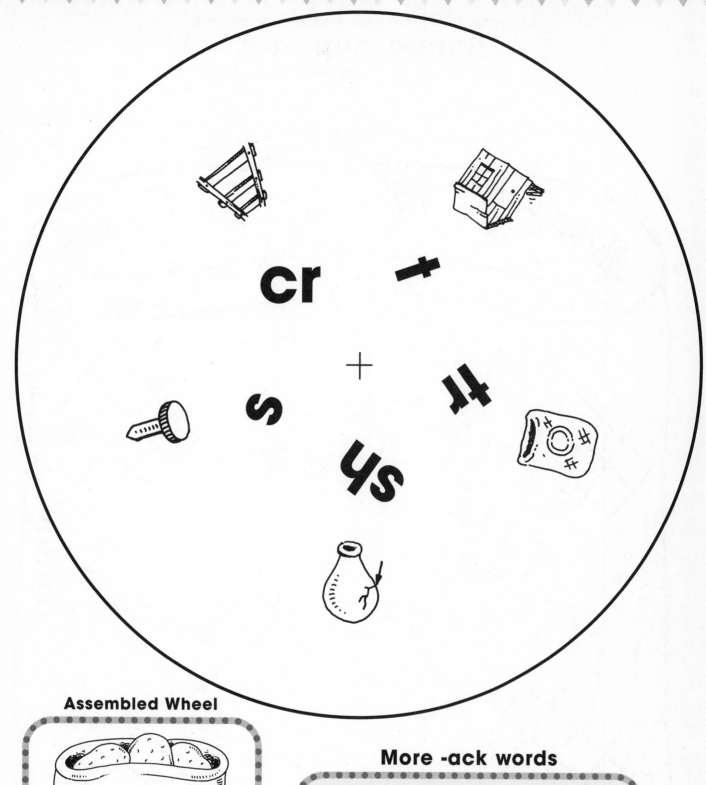

Assembled Wheel

s ack

More -ack words

hack	quack	slack
Jack	rack	smack
lack	black	snack
Mack	clack	stack
pack	knack	whack

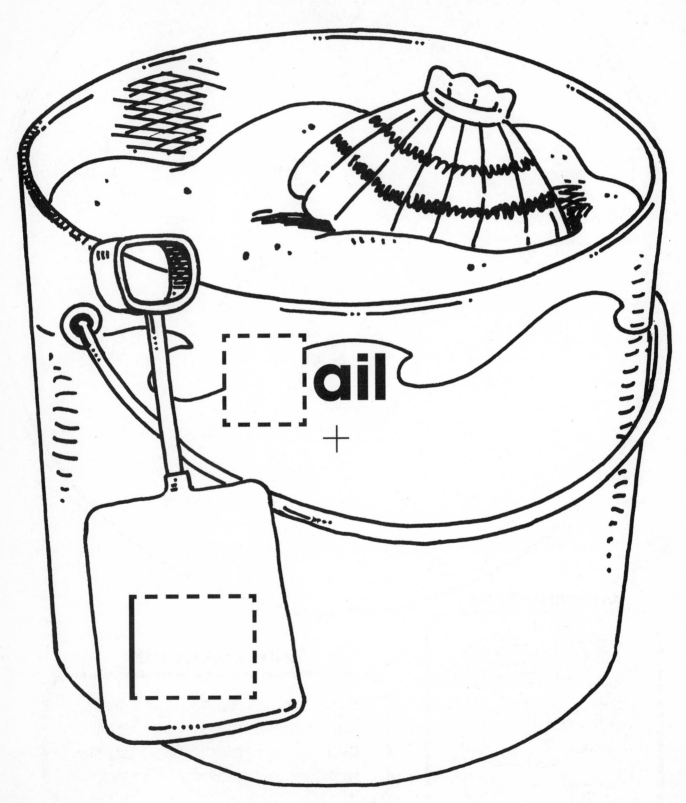

ail
+

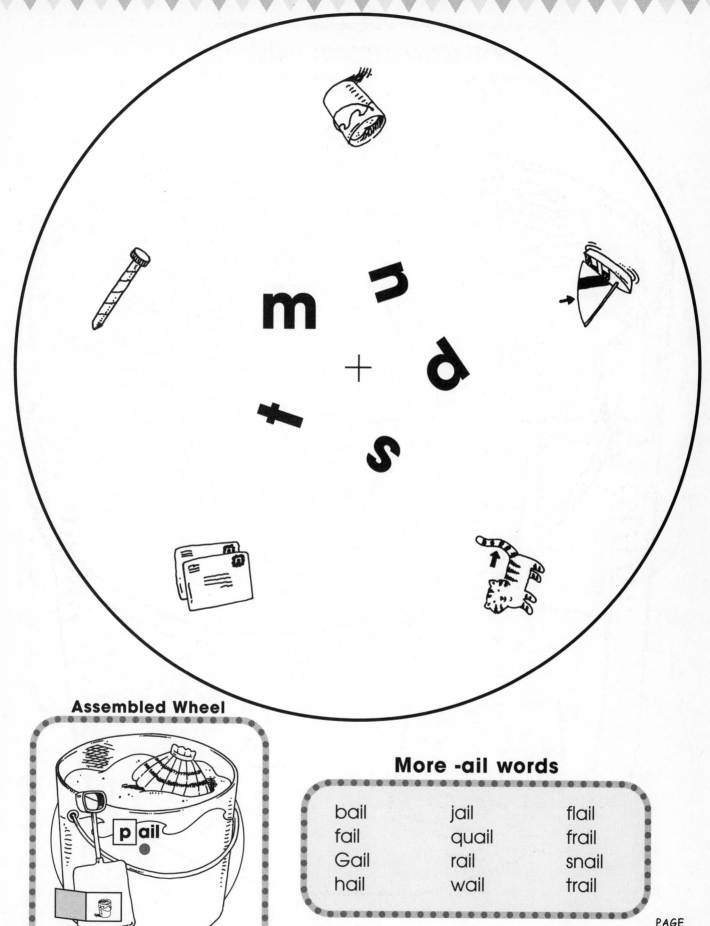

Assembled Wheel

p ail

More -ail words

bail	jail	flail
fail	quail	frail
Gail	rail	snail
hail	wail	trail

PAGE
15

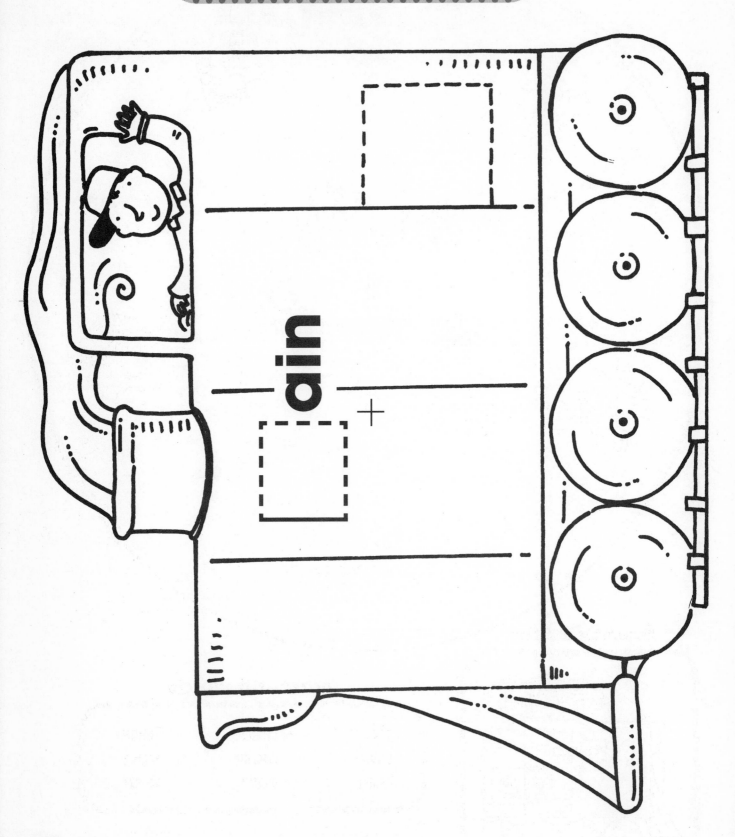

ain

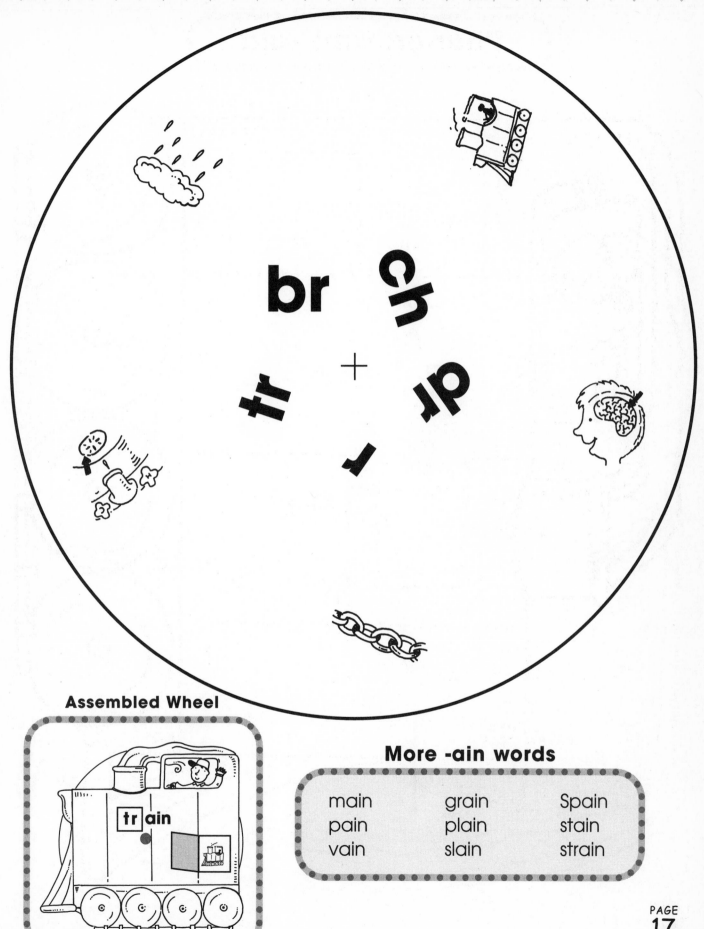

br ch

+

tr dr

r

Assembled Wheel

tr ain

More -ain words

main	grain	Spain
pain	plain	stain
vain	slain	strain

Phonogram: -ake

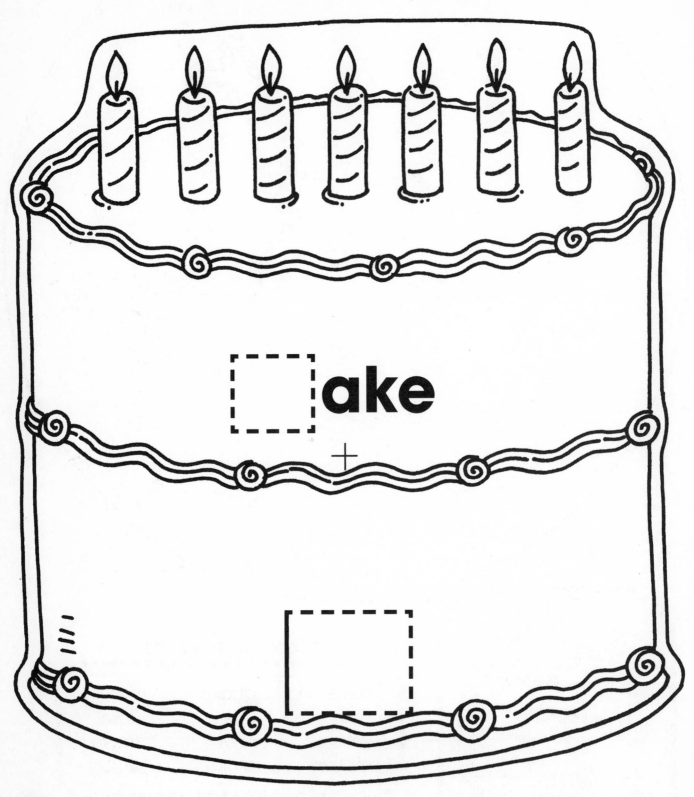

ake

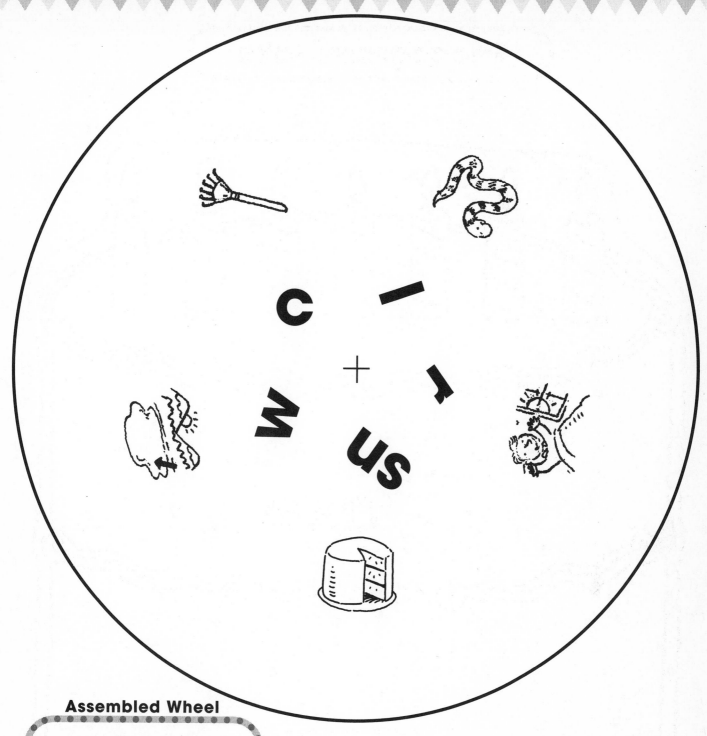

Assembled Wheel

c ake

More -ake words

bake	quake	drake
fake	sake	flake
Jake	take	shake
make	brake	stake

ale

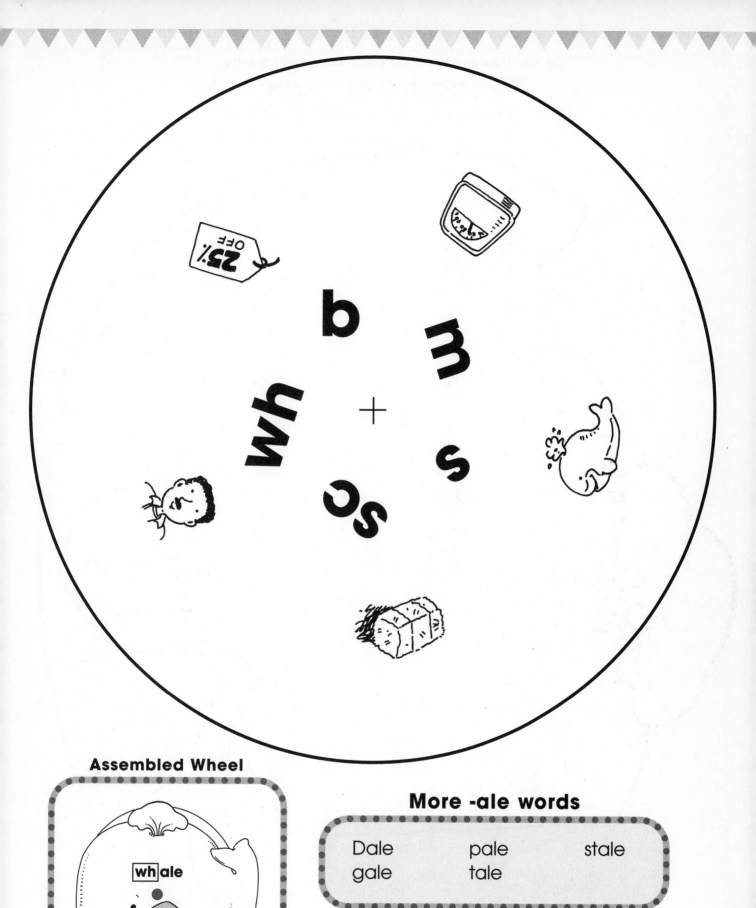

Assembled Wheel

wh ale

More -ale words

| Dale | pale | stale |
| gale | tale | |

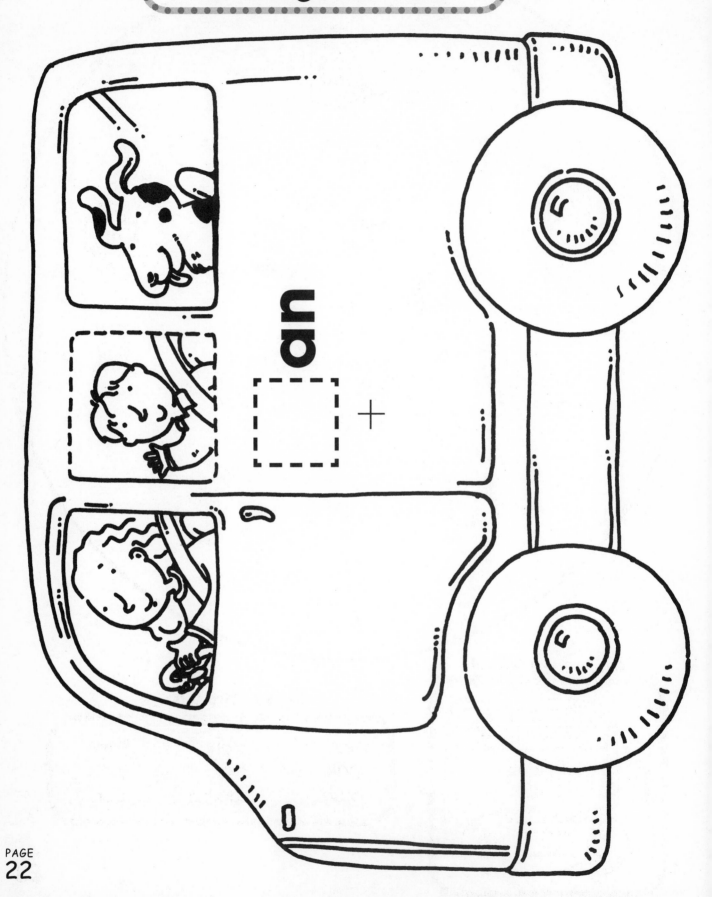

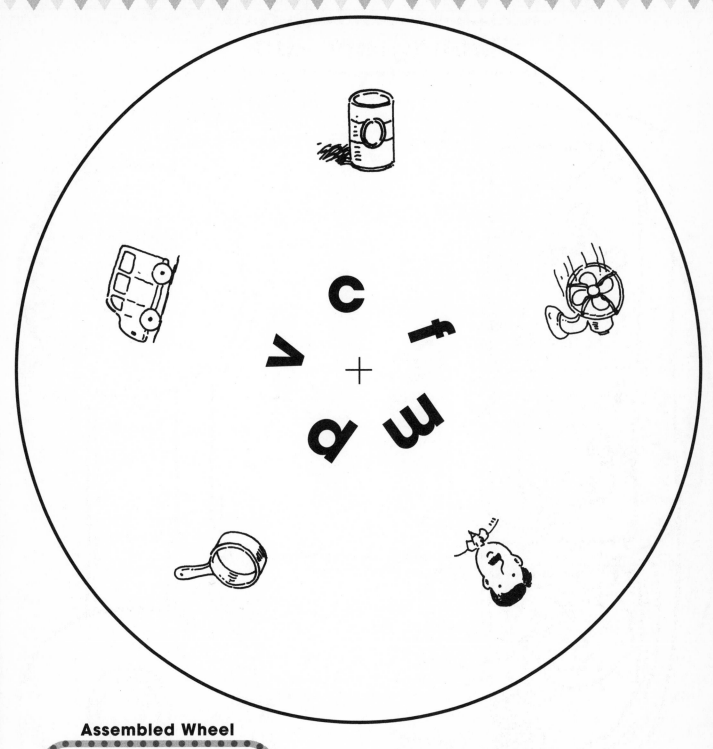

Assembled Wheel

v an

More -an words

ban	clan	Stan
Dan	plan	span
bran	scan	than

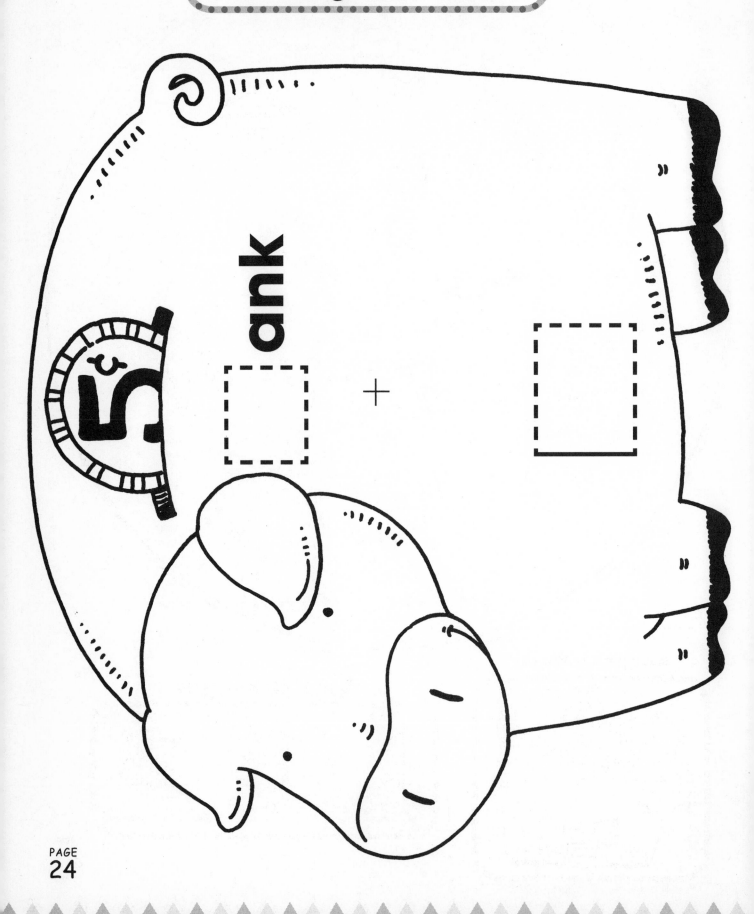

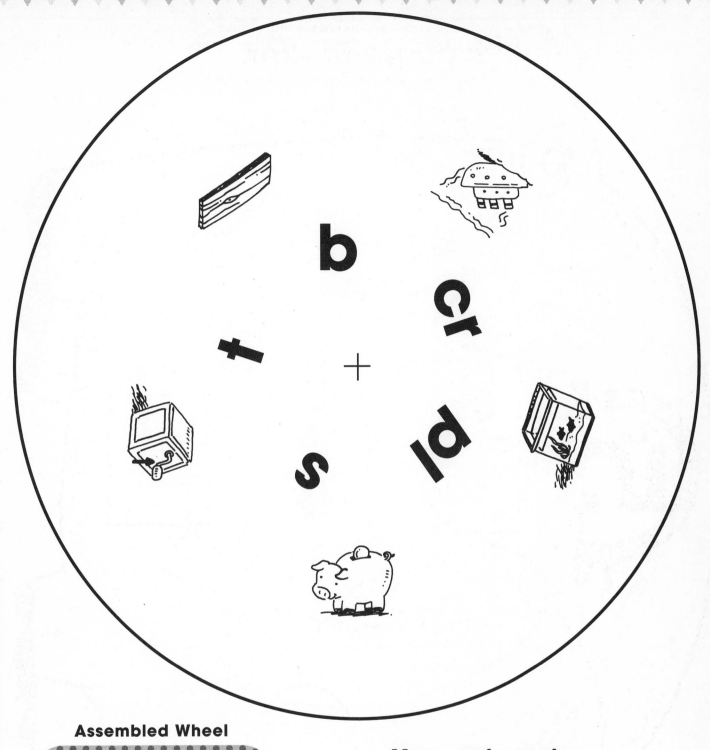

Assembled Wheel

More -ank words

Hank	clank	prank
lank	drank	spank
rank	flank	stank
yank	Frank	

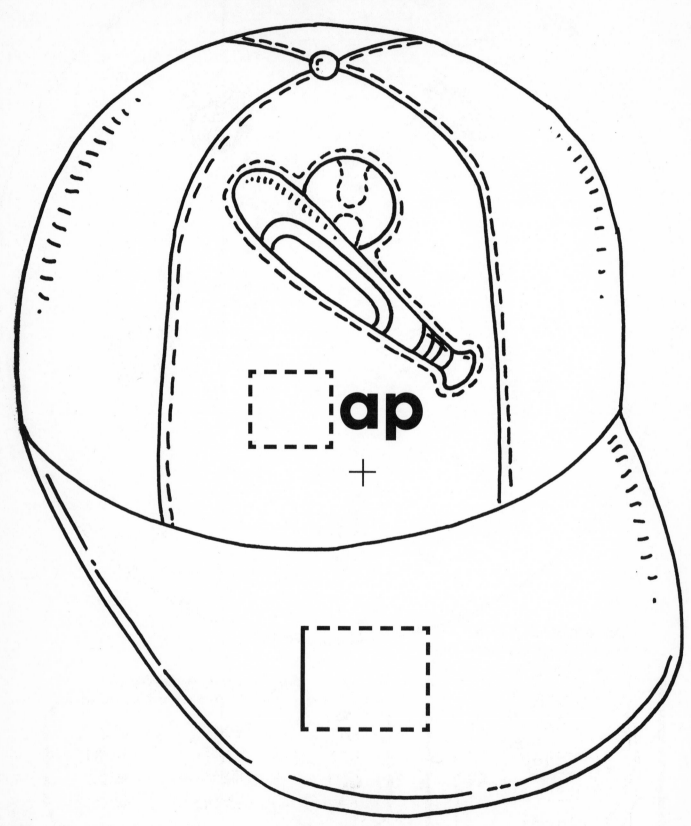

ap

+

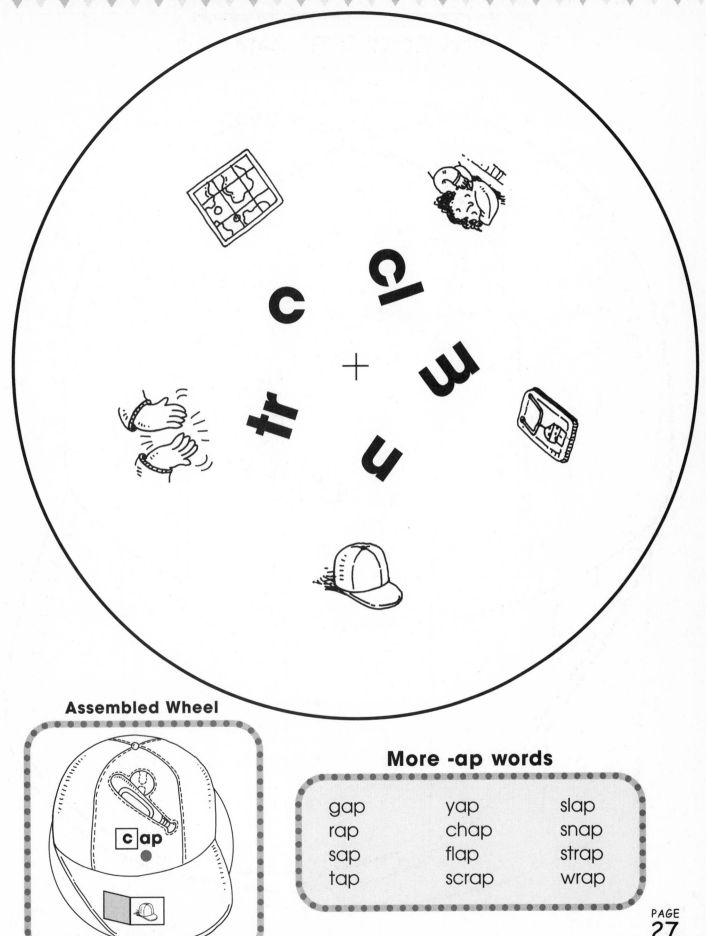

Assembled Wheel

c ap

More -ap words

gap	yap	slap
rap	chap	snap
sap	flap	strap
tap	scrap	wrap

Phonogram: -ash

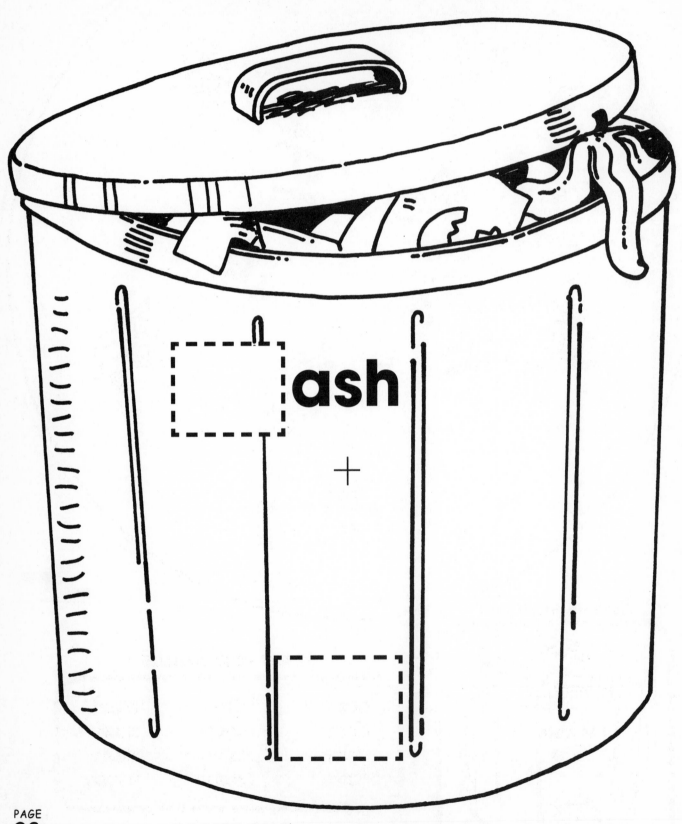

ash

+

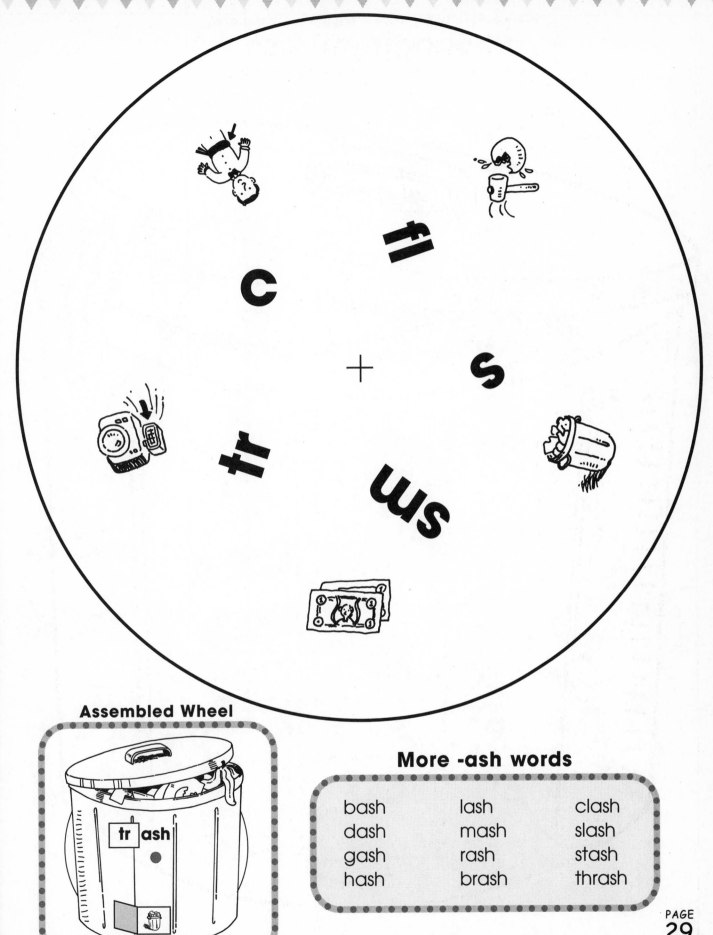

Assembled Wheel

More -ash words

bash	lash	clash
dash	mash	slash
gash	rash	stash
hash	brash	thrash

at

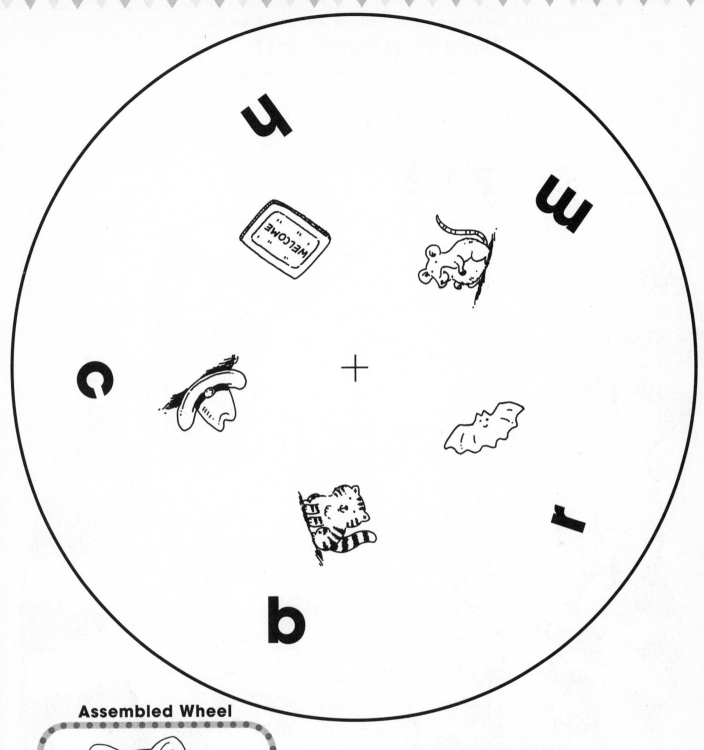

Assembled Wheel

More -at words

fat	vat	scat
gnat	brat	slat
pat	chat	spat
sat	flat	that

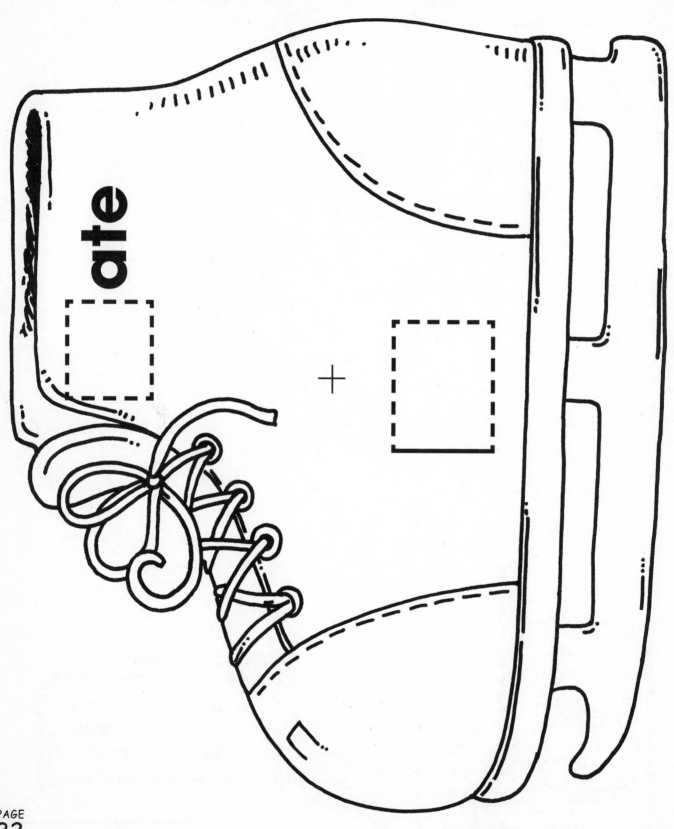

ate

+

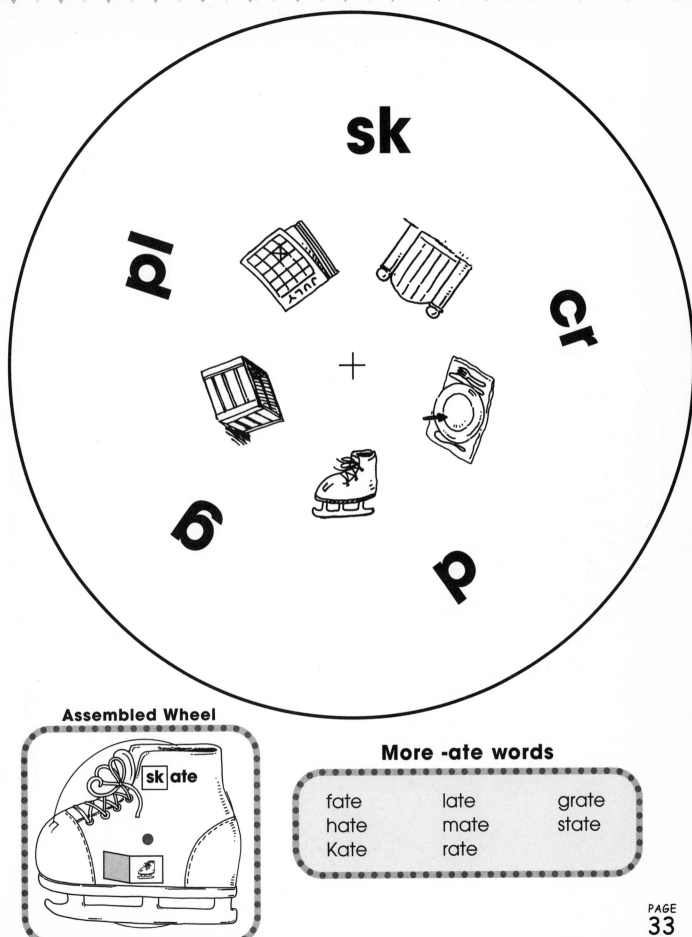

sk

pl

cr

g

p

+

Assembled Wheel

sk ate

More -ate words

fate	late	grate
hate	mate	state
Kate	rate	

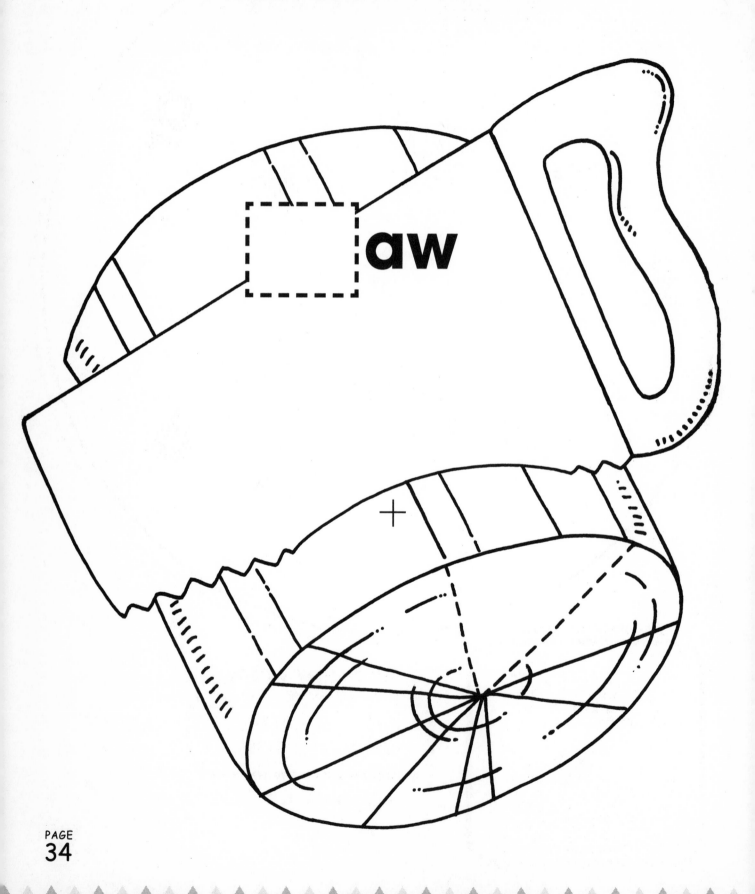

aw

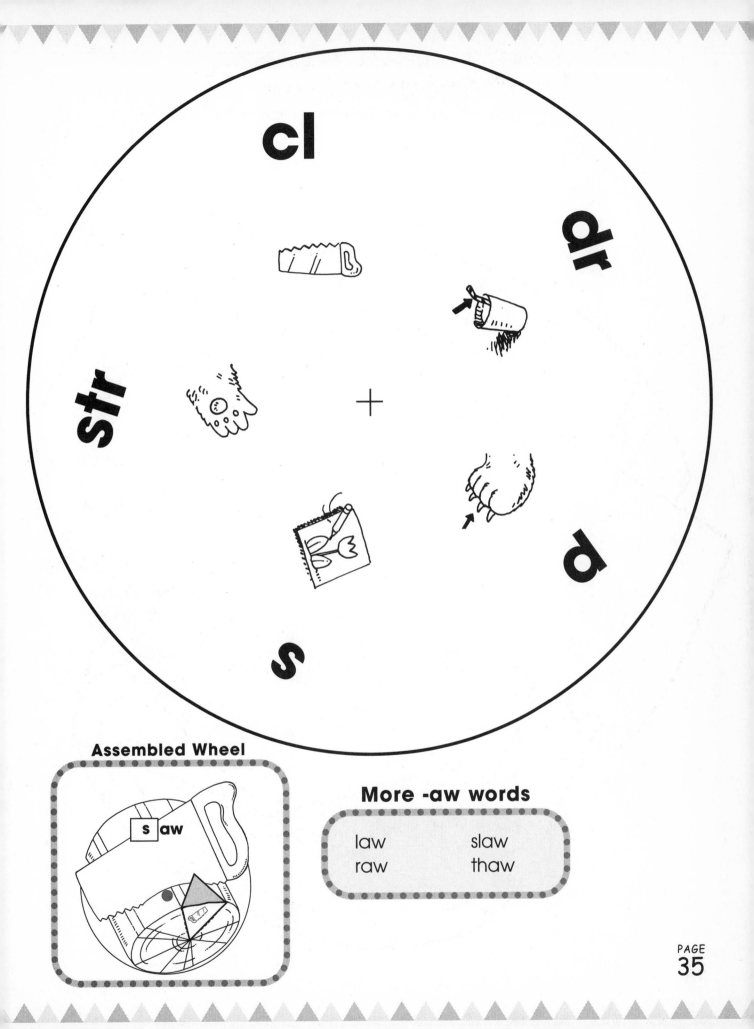

cl

dr

str

d

s

+

Assembled Wheel

s aw

More -aw words

law   slaw
raw   thaw

Phonogram: -ay

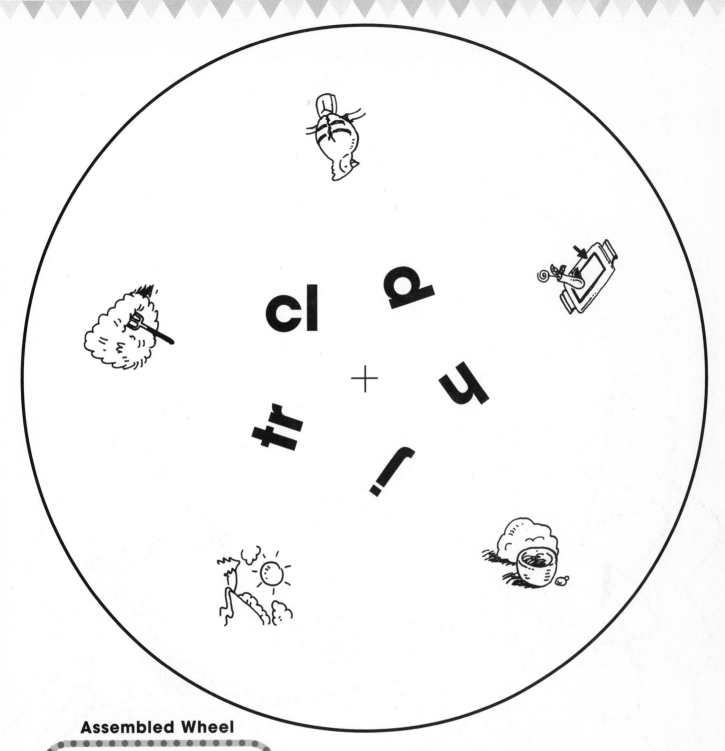

Assembled Wheel

More -ay words

bay	ray	slay
gay	say	spray
lay	way	stay
may	fray	stray
nay	gray	sway
pay	pray	

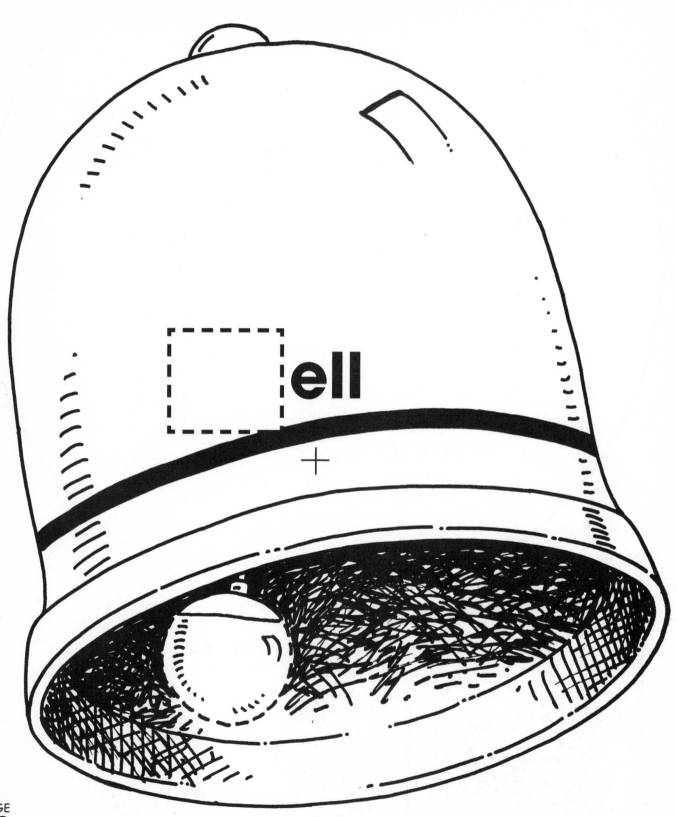

ell

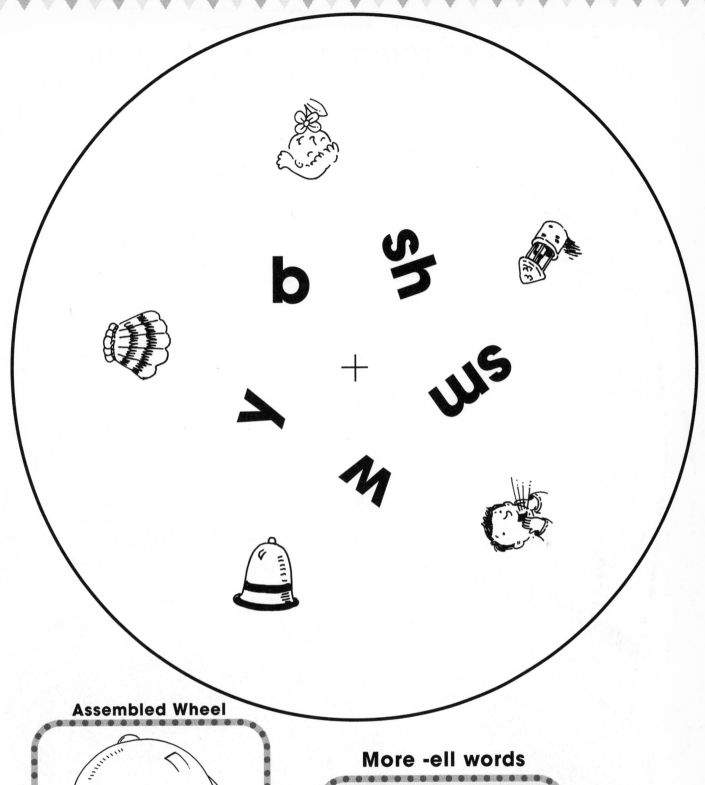

Assembled Wheel

b ell

More -ell words

cell	sell
dell	tell
fell	dwell
jell	spell
Nell	swell

est

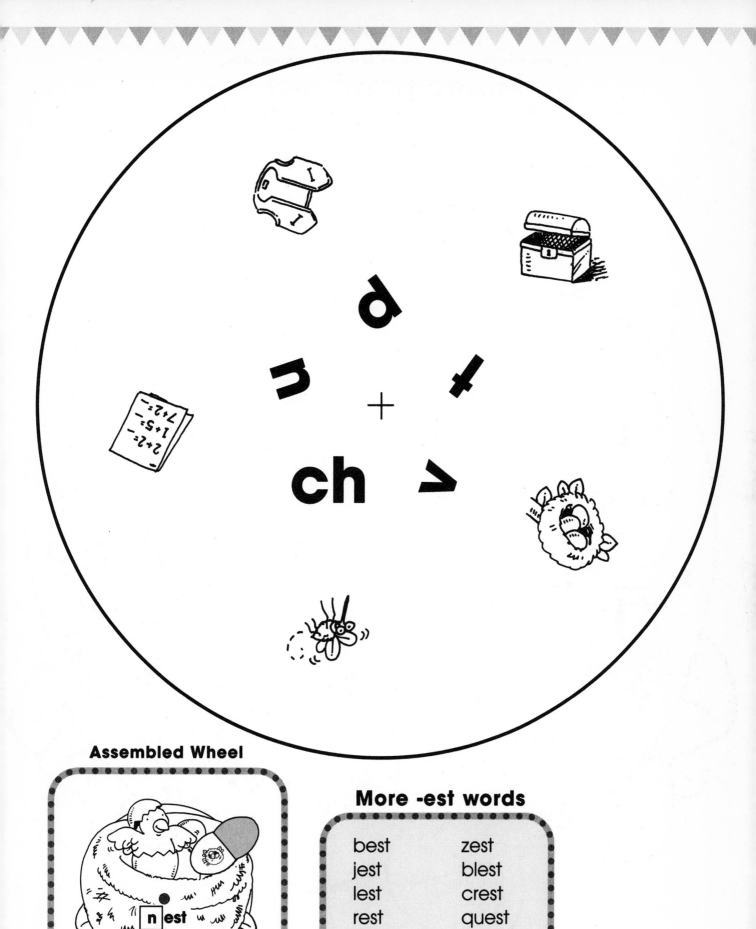

Assembled Wheel

More -est words

best	zest
jest	blest
lest	crest
rest	quest
west	wrest

Phonogram: -ice

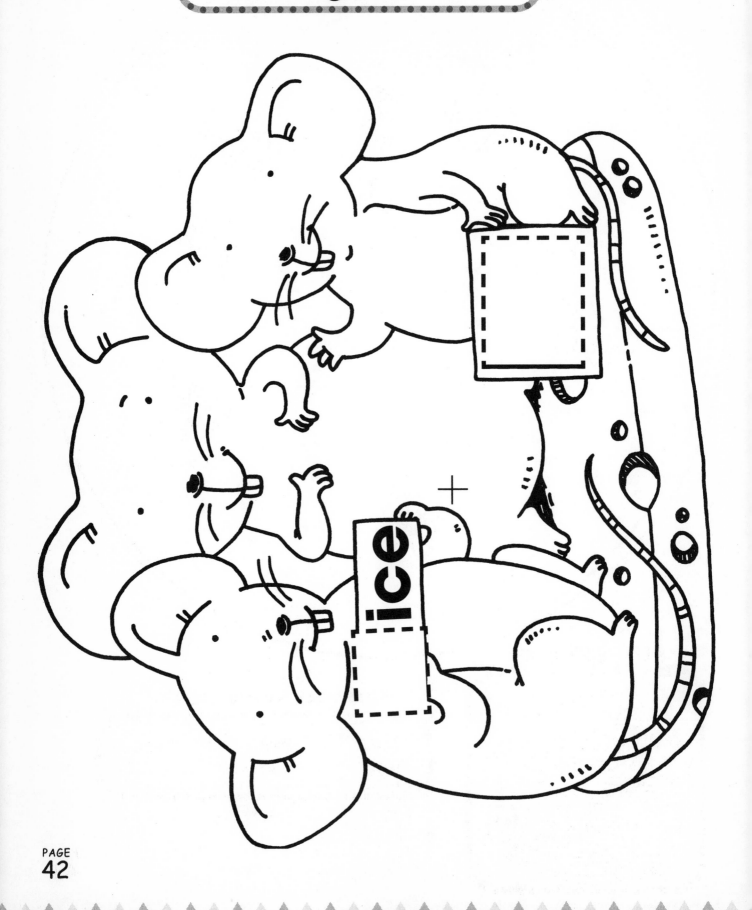

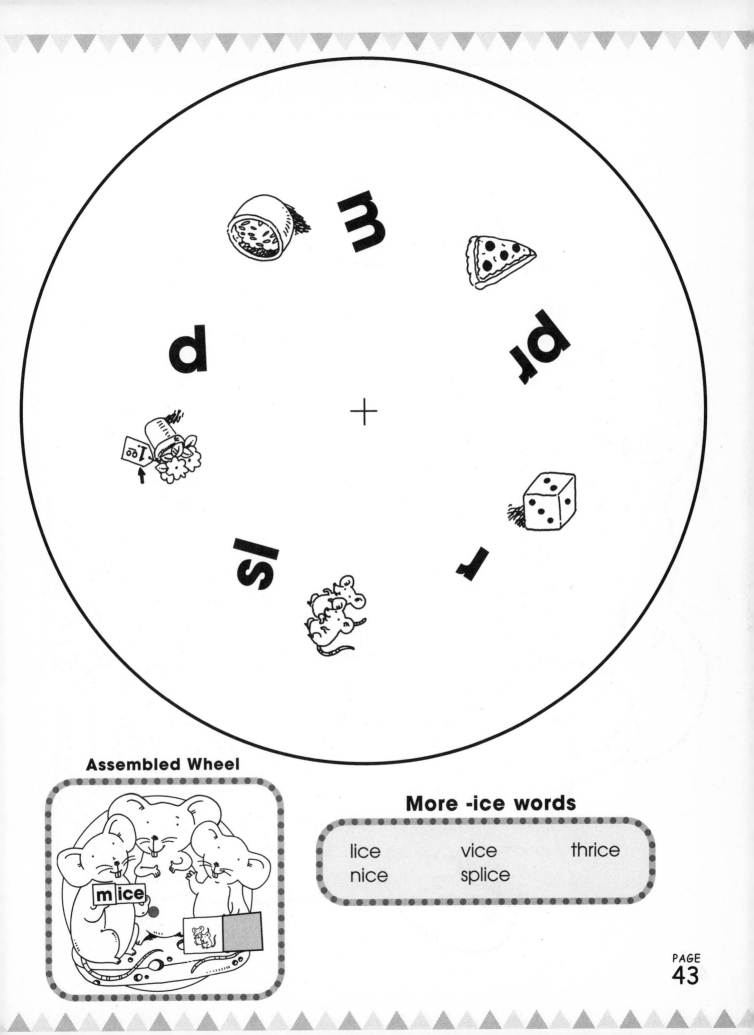

Assembled Wheel

More -ice words

lice	vice	thrice
nice	splice	

Phonogram: -ick

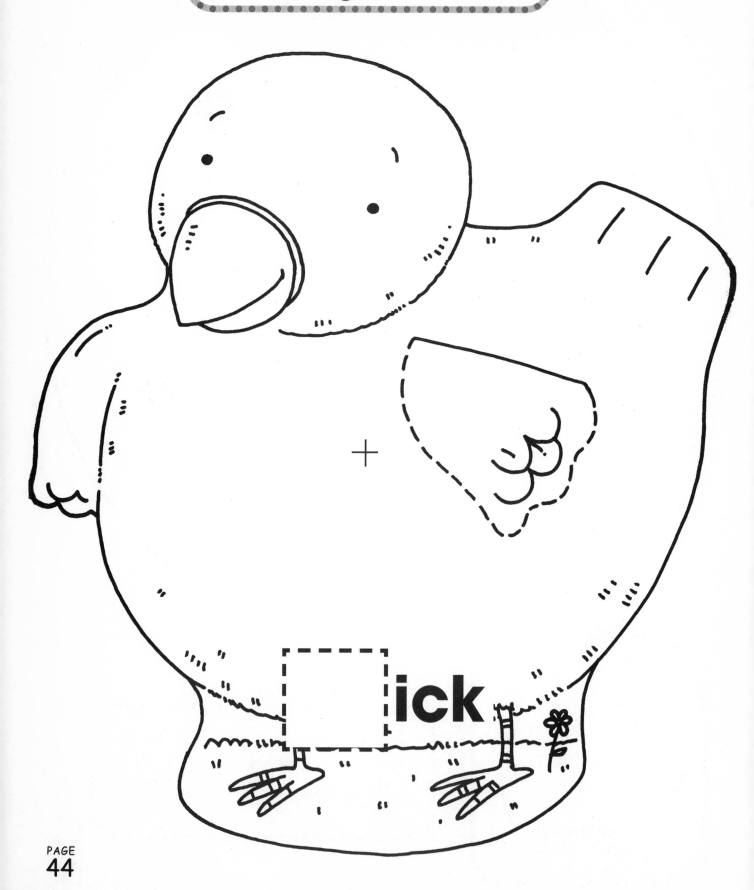

ick

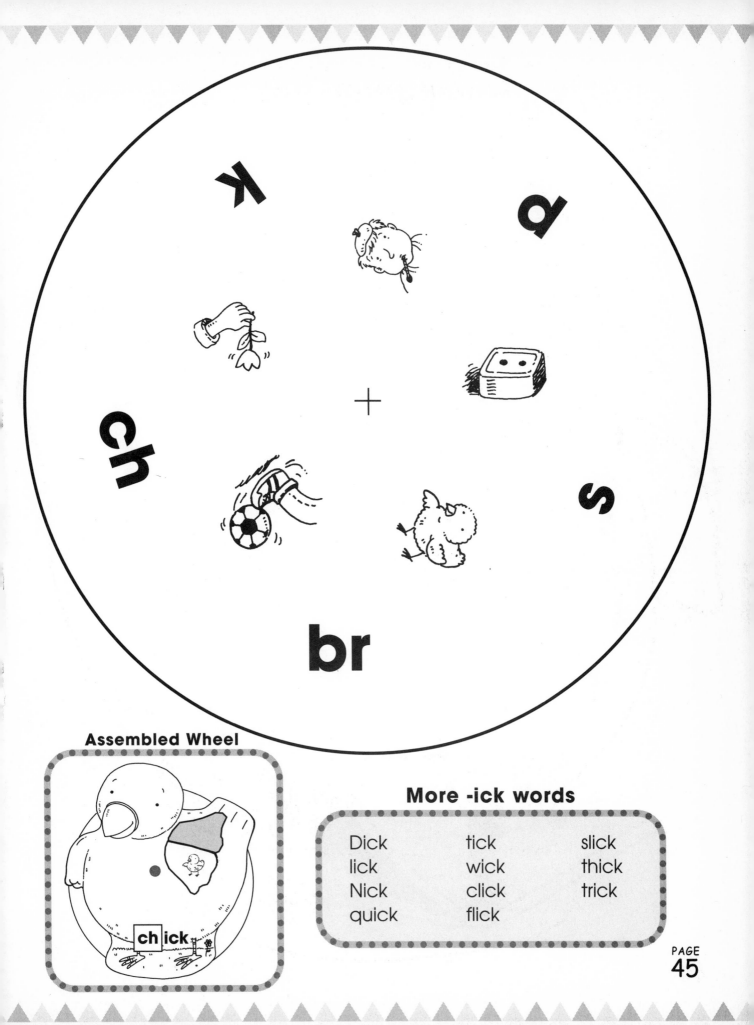

Assembled Wheel

More -ick words

Dick	tick	slick
lick	wick	thick
Nick	click	trick
quick	flick	

ide

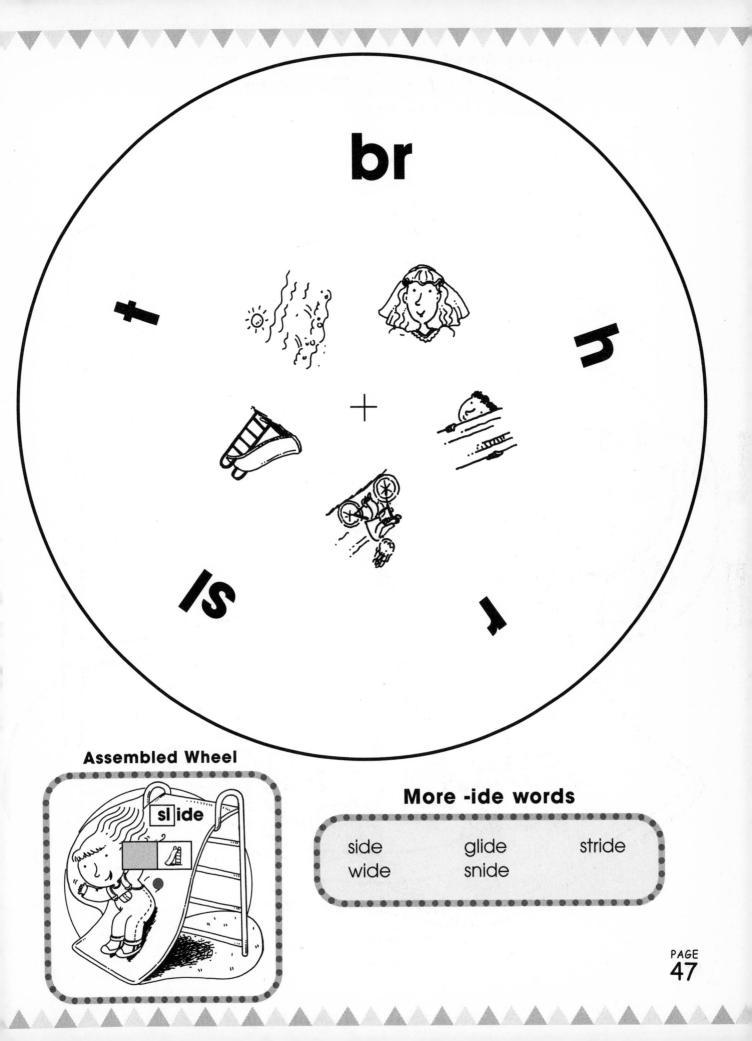

br

Assembled Wheel

sl**ide**

More -ide words

side	glide	stride
wide	snide	

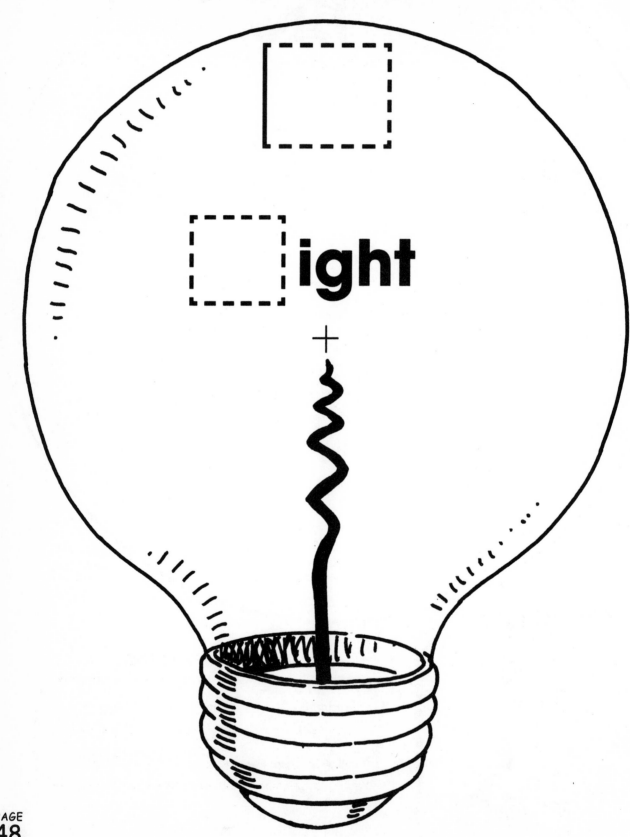

ight

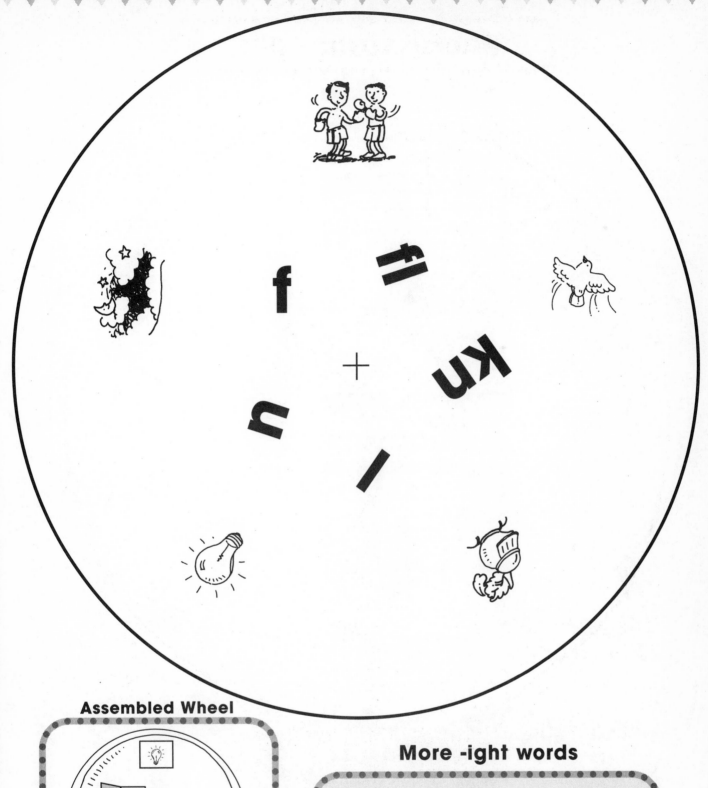

f
fl
kn
n
l
+

Assembled Wheel

l ight

More -ight words

might	tight	fright
right	blight	plight
sight	bright	slight

Phonogram: -ill

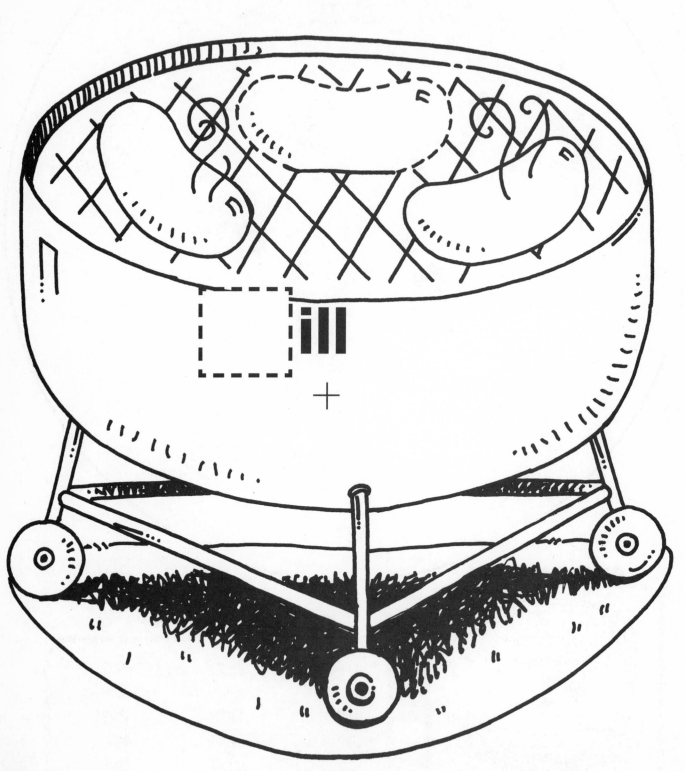

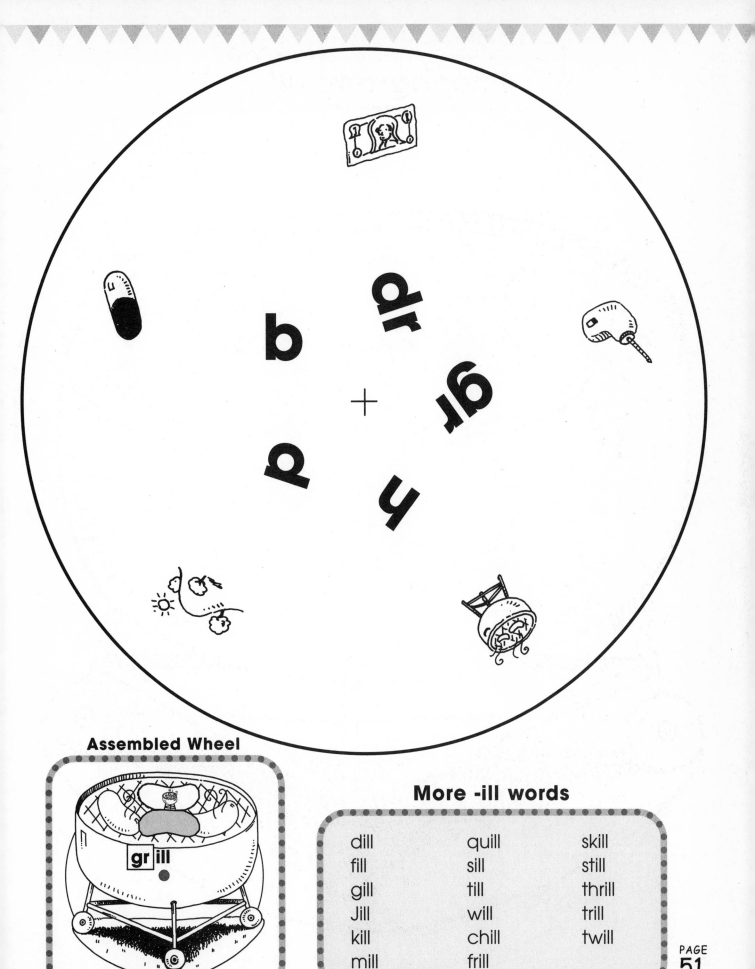

Assembled Wheel

gr ill

More -ill words

dill	quill	skill
fill	sill	still
gill	till	thrill
Jill	will	trill
kill	chill	twill
mill	frill	

Phonogram: -in

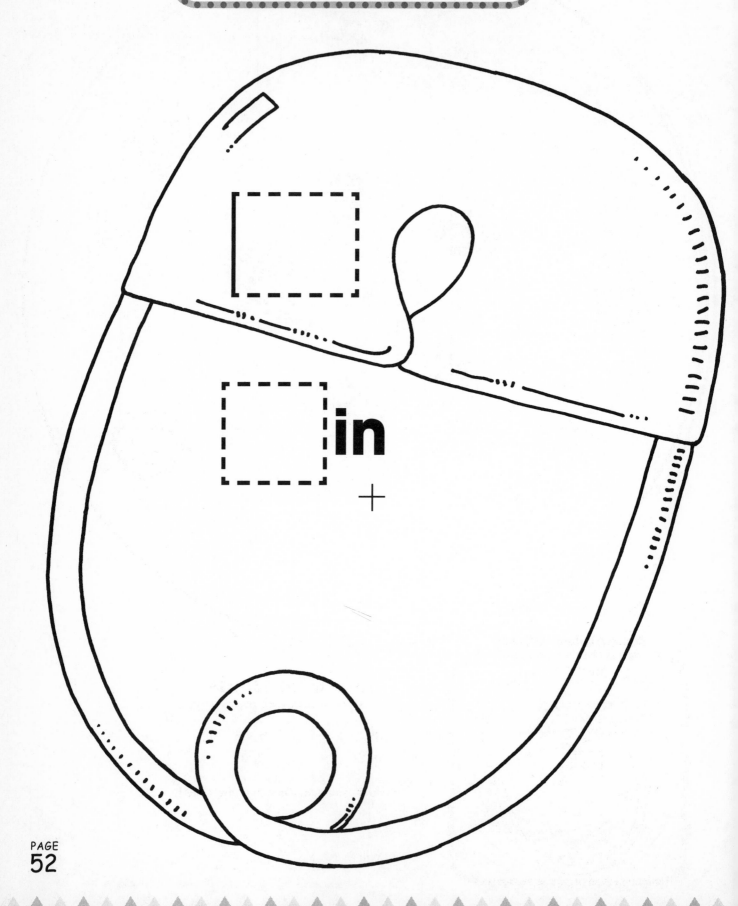

in

+

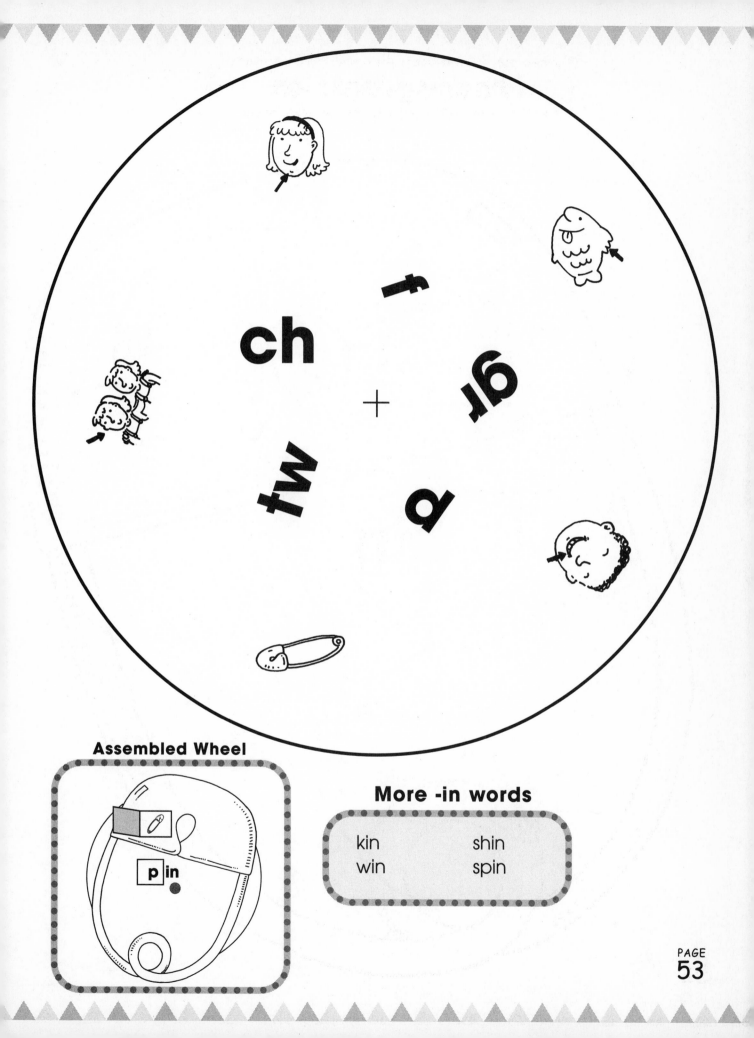

Assembled Wheel

p in

More -in words

kin	shin
win	spin

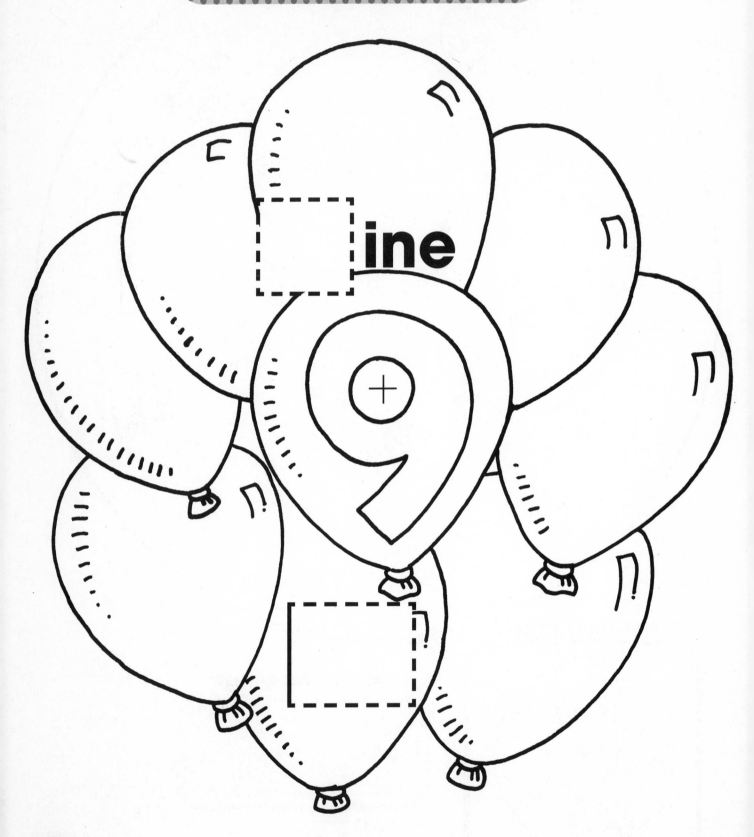

ine

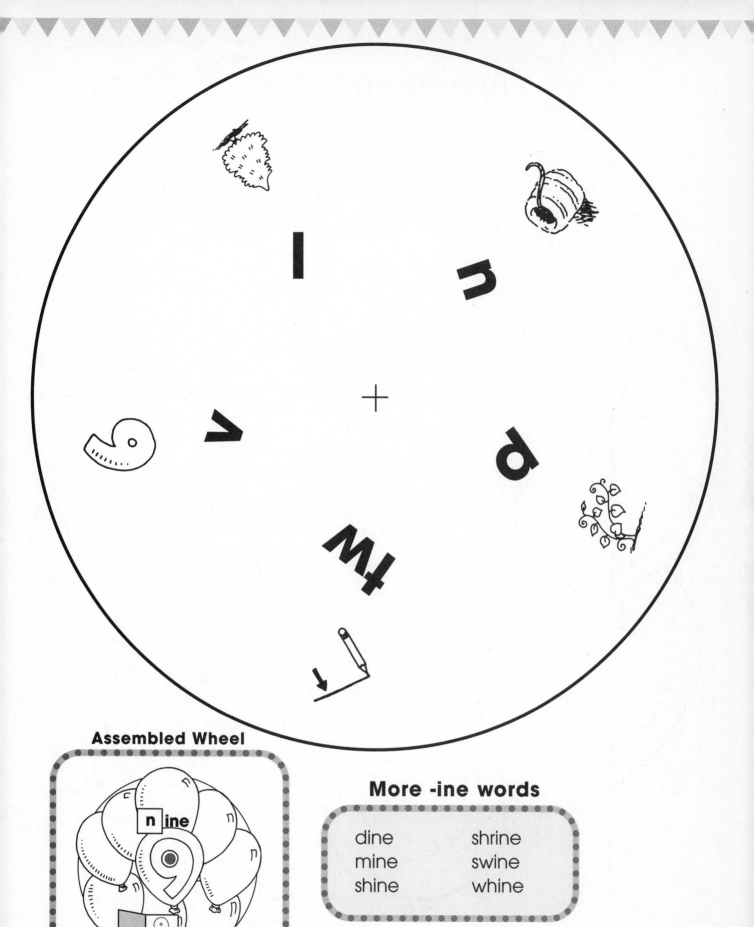

Assembled Wheel

More -ine words

dine	shrine
mine	swine
shine	whine

Phonogram: -ing

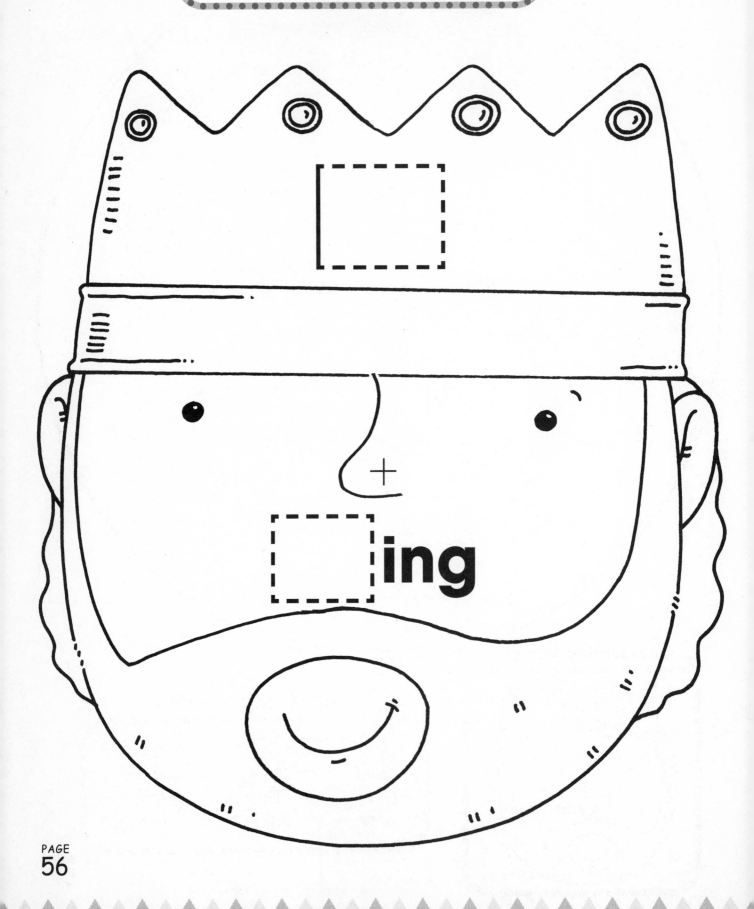

ing

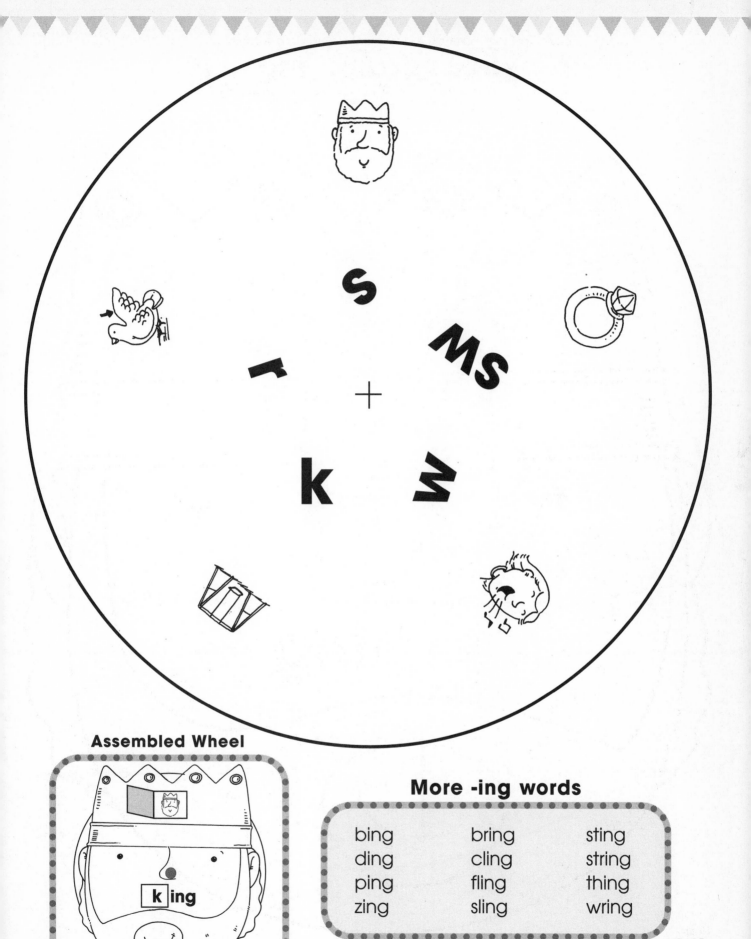

Assembled Wheel

k ing

More -ing words

bing	bring	sting
ding	cling	string
ping	fling	thing
zing	sling	wring

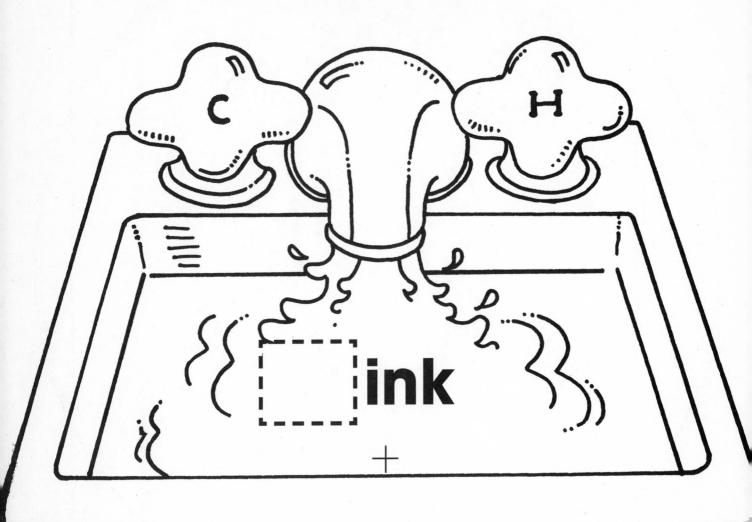

ink

+

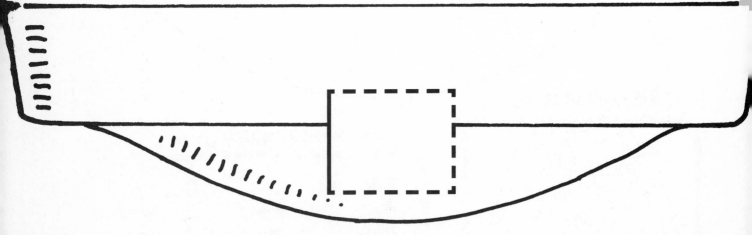

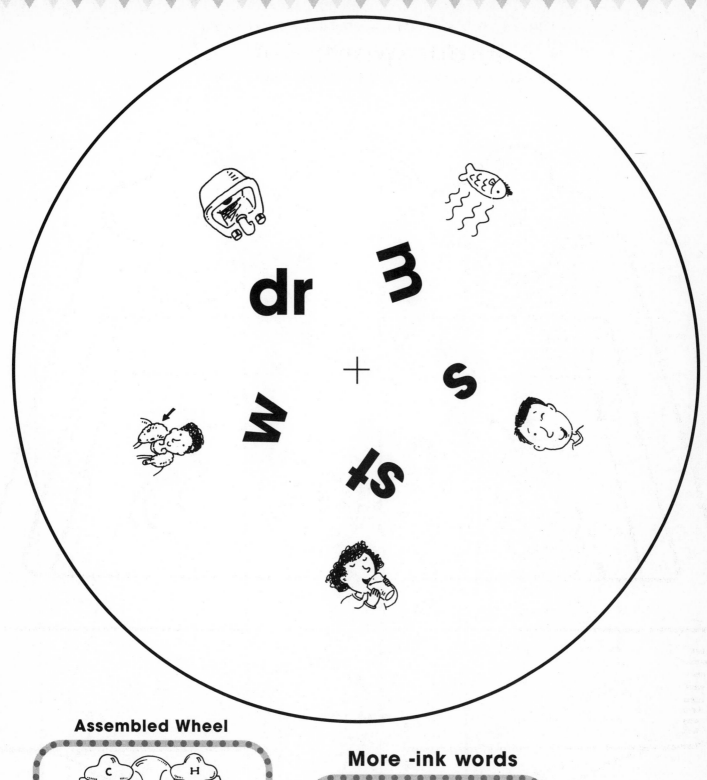

dr ʒ

+

w s

st

Assembled Wheel

More -ink words

kink	pink
link	rink
blink	shrink
brink	slink
clink	think

Phonogram: -ip

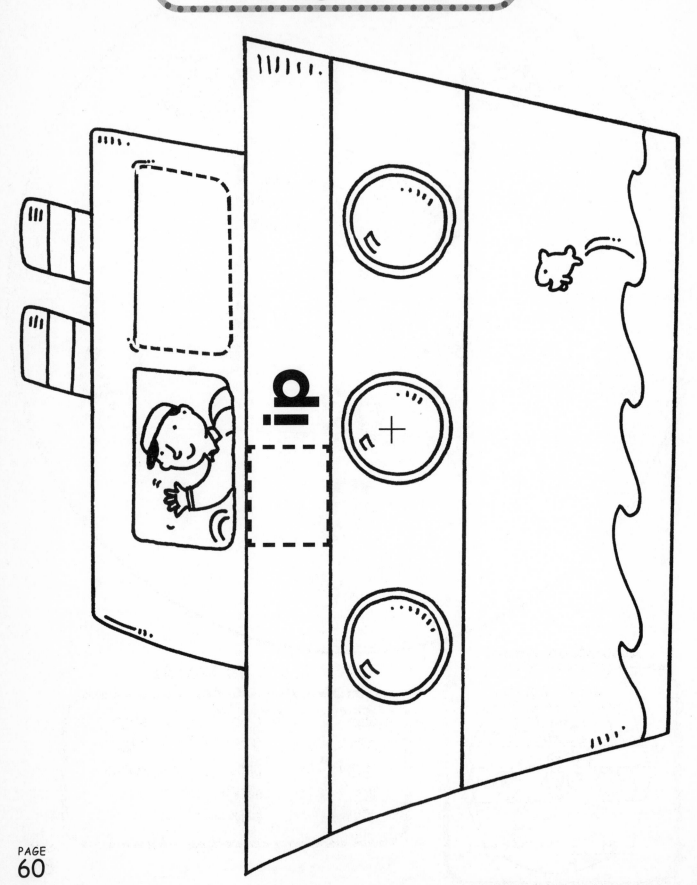

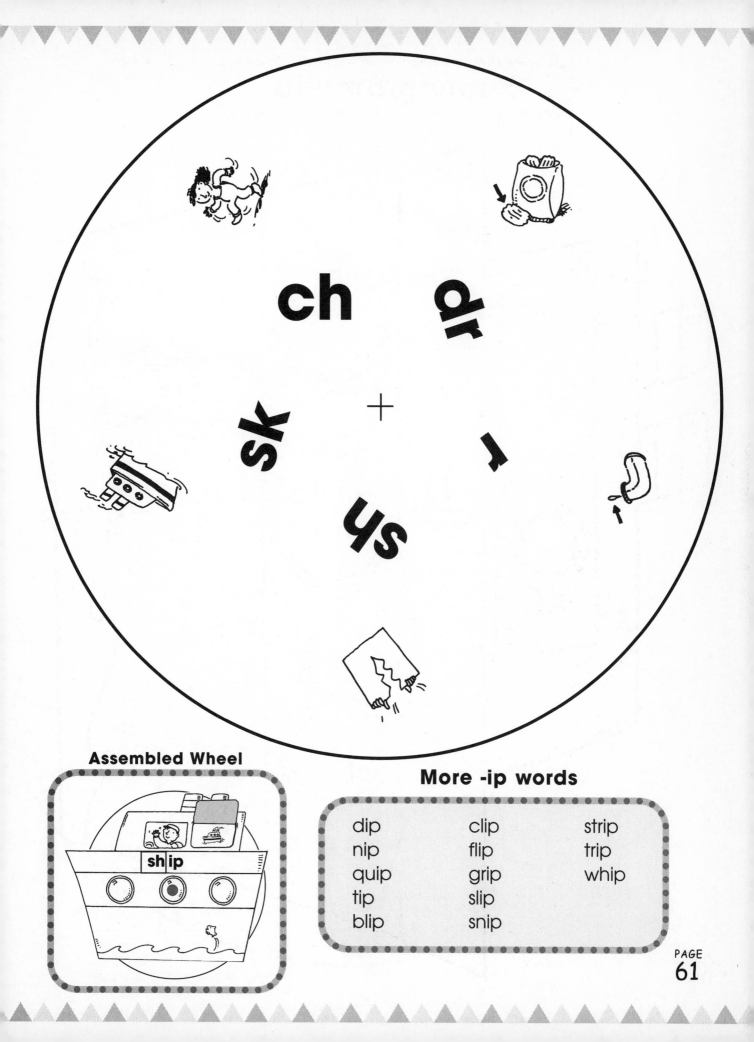

ch   dr

sk   +   r

sh

Assembled Wheel

sh|ip

More -ip words

dip	clip	strip
nip	flip	trip
quip	grip	whip
tip	slip	
blip	snip	

Phonogram: -ock

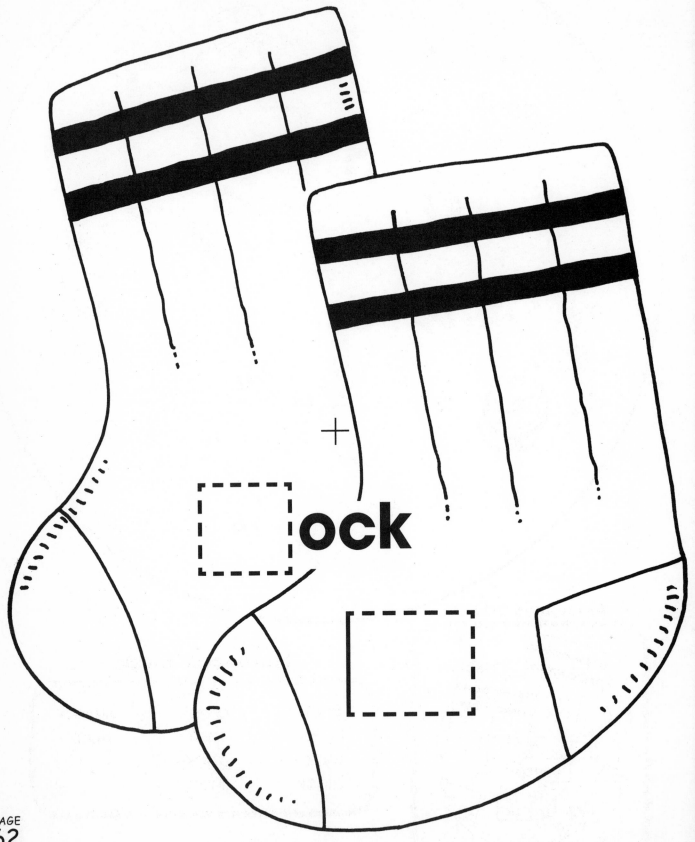

ock

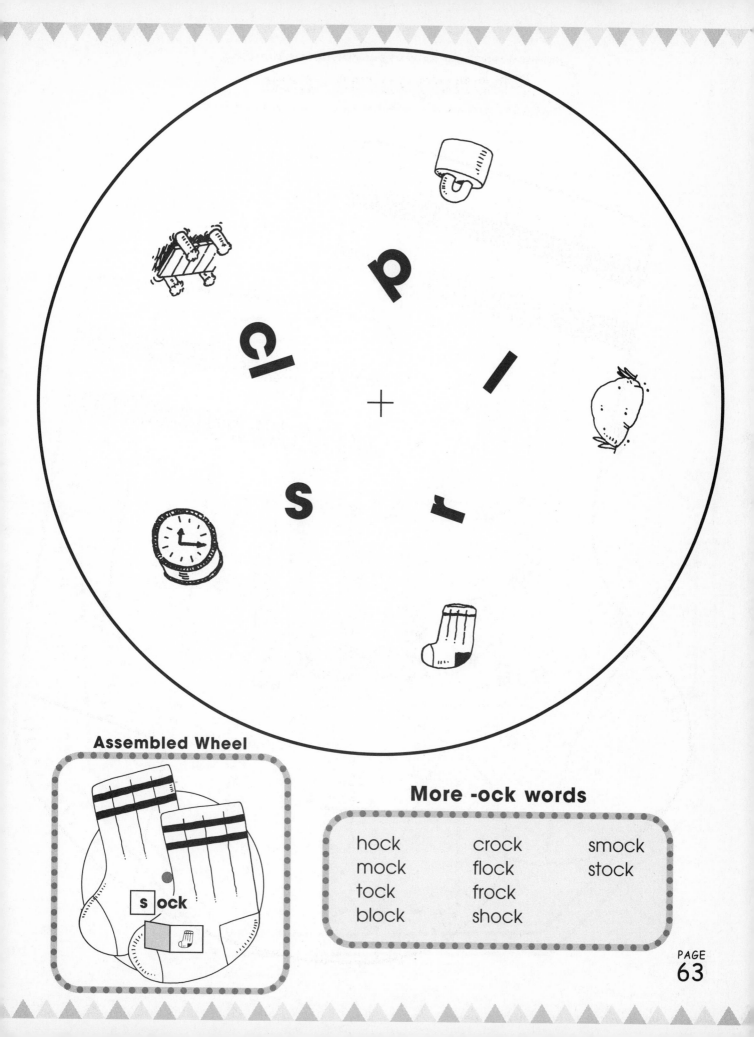

cl **p** **l** **s** **r** +

Assembled Wheel

s **ock**

More -ock words

hock	crock	smock
mock	flock	stock
tock	frock	
block	shock	

Phonogram: -op

op

STOP

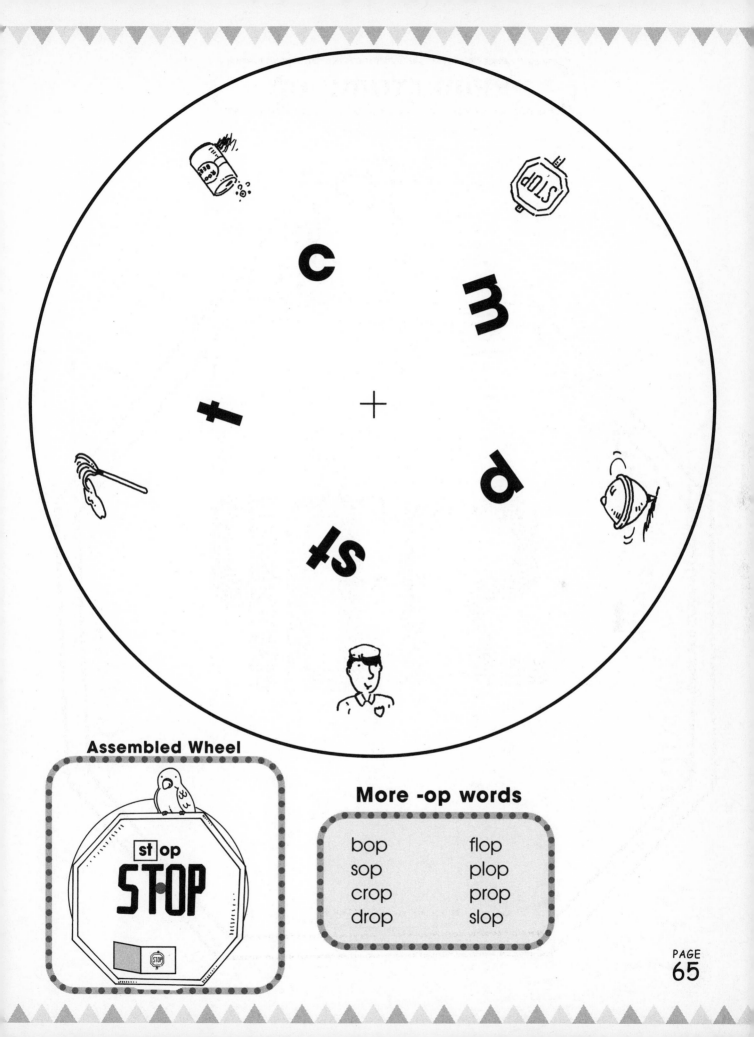

Assembled Wheel

st op
STOP

More -op words

bop	flop
sop	plop
crop	prop
drop	slop

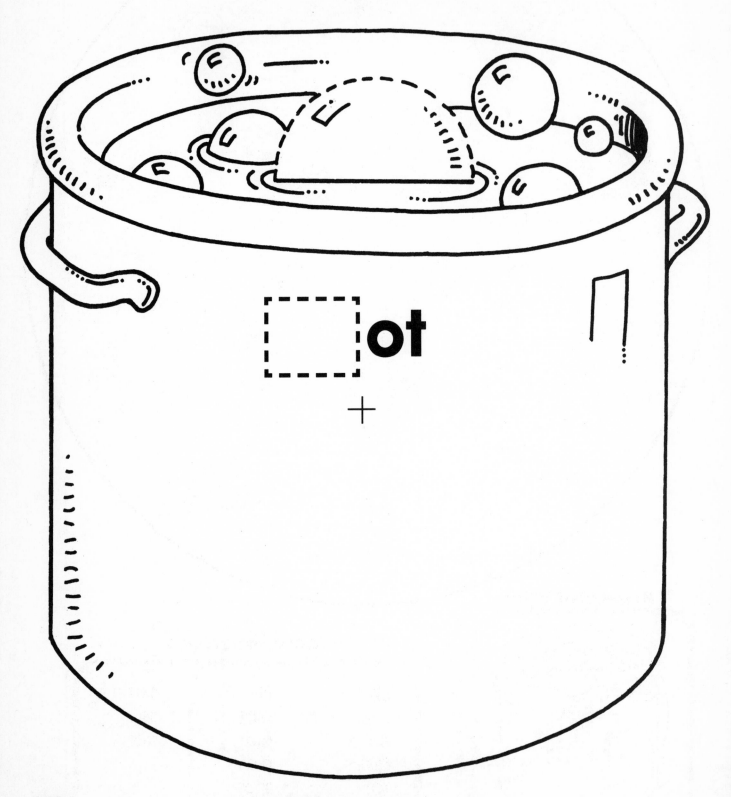

ot

+

Assembled Wheel

p ot

More -ot words

got	tot	slot
jot	blot	spot
lot	clot	trot
not	plot	
rot	shot	

uck

+

Phonogram: -uck

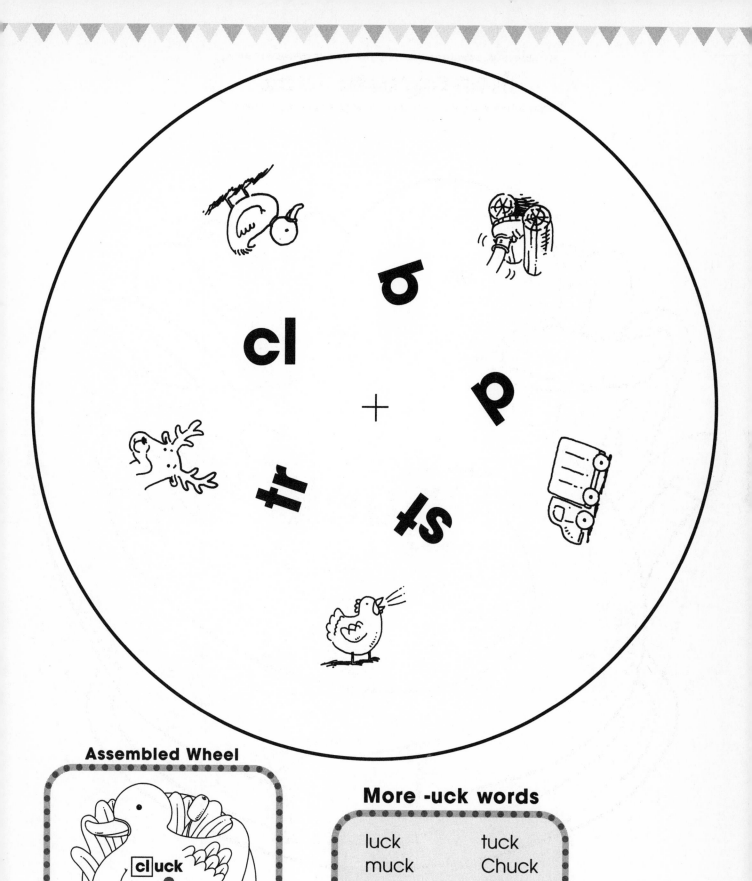

Assembled Wheel

cl uck

More -uck words

luck	tuck
muck	Chuck
puck	pluck
suck	yuck

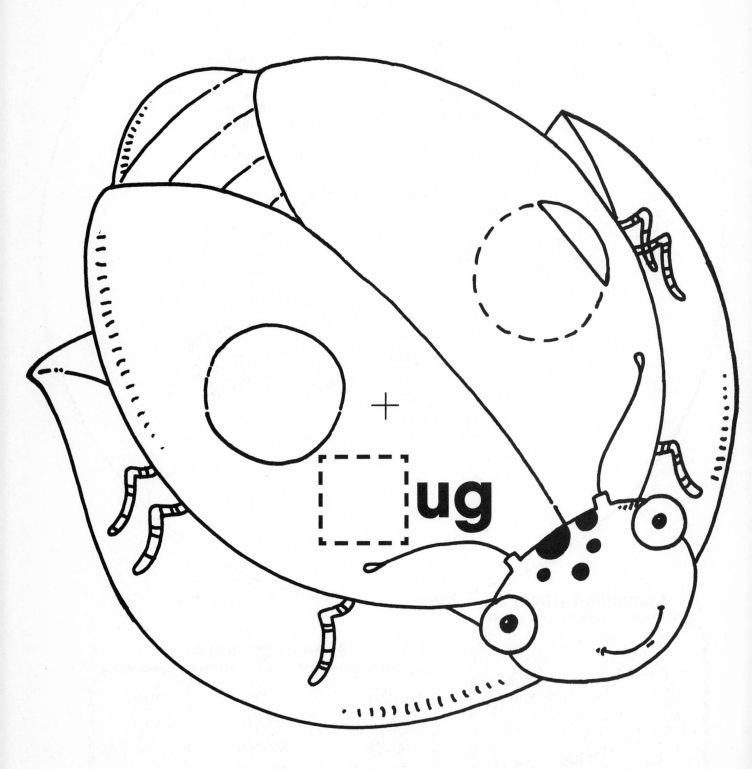

$+$

☐ ug

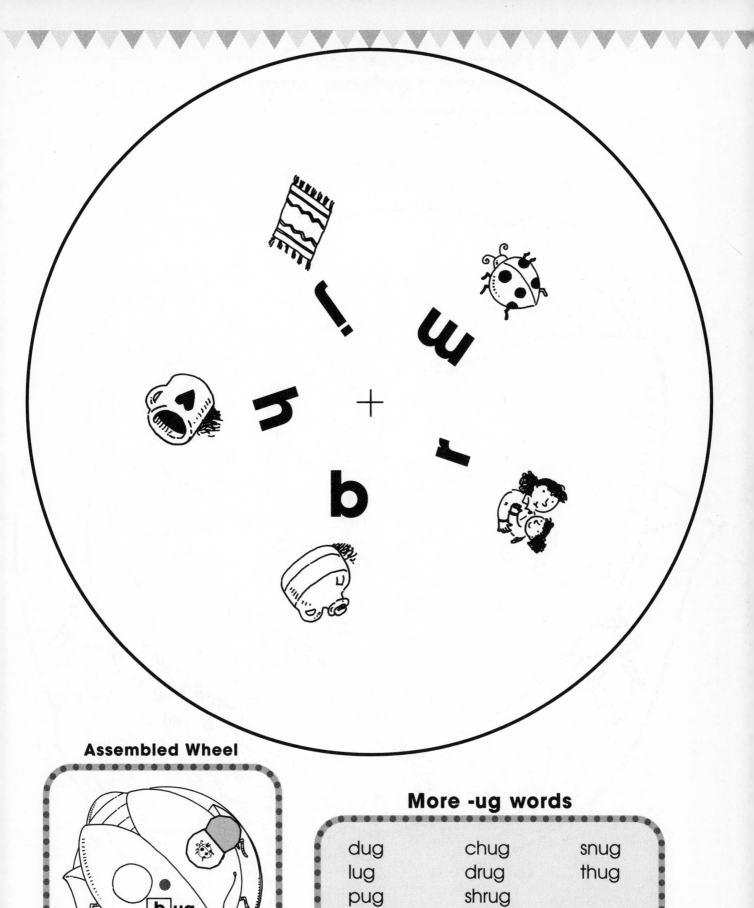

Assembled Wheel

More -ug words

dug	chug	snug
lug	drug	thug
pug	shrug	
trug	smug	

Phonogram: -ump

ump

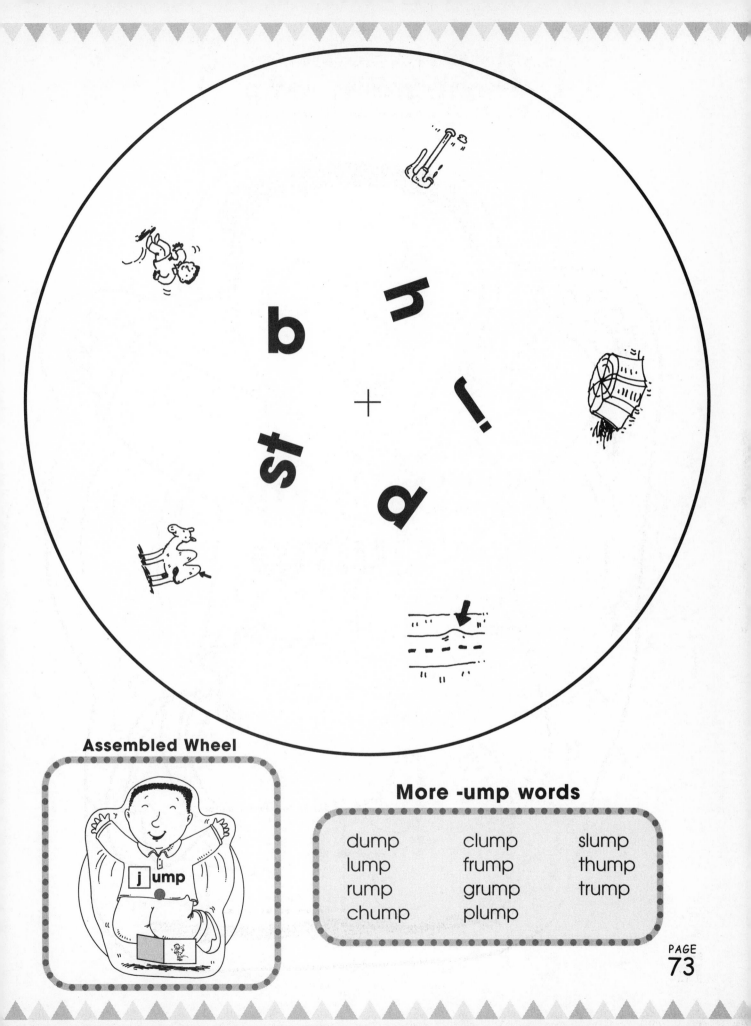

Assembled Wheel

More -ump words

dump	clump	slump
lump	frump	thump
rump	grump	trump
chump	plump	

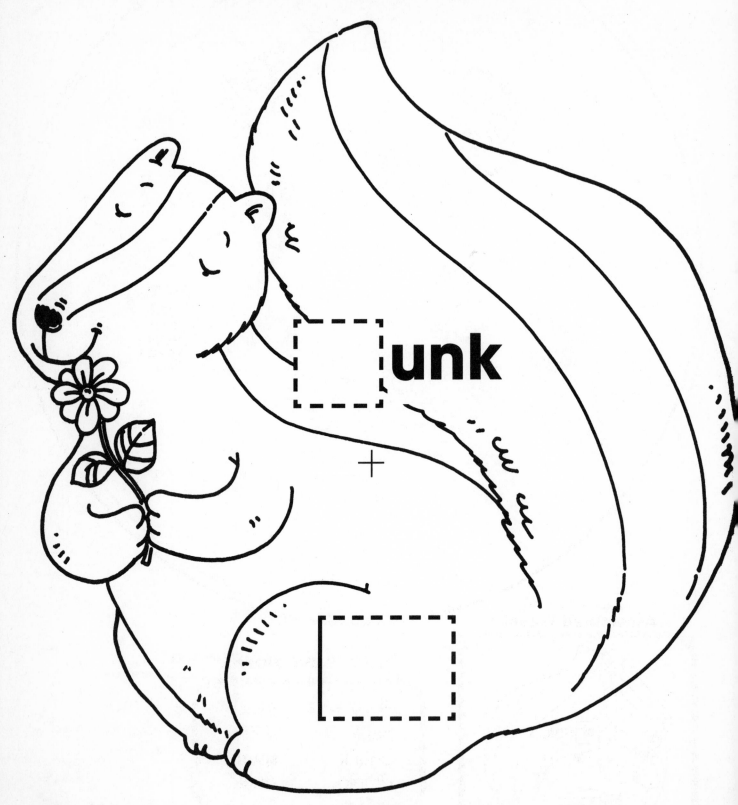

unk

Assembled Wheel

More -unk words

dunk	flunk
hunk	slunk
chunk	spunk
drunk	stunk

Notes

Notes

Notes

Notes

Notes

DATE DUE			
			PRINTED IN U.S.A.